Buy the Right Horse

A step by step guide to ask the right questions, avoid mistakes and buy with confidence.

Jeanette Gower

PLATYPUS
PUBLISHING

Platypus Publishing

Cover photo by Roger Foster.
Avah Bowen on Chalani Surprise.
– happy horse, happy teenager.

Note:
For simplification purposes, the following text
will use "he," "him" and "his" to indicate all genders.

PLATYPUS
PUBLISHING

Paperback: 978-1-965016-64-0
Hardcover: 978-1-965016-65-7

First edition published in Australia March 25.

Contents

Introduction

Buying a horse should be an exciting adventure, but often it feels like navigating a maze blindfolded. You may be caught in the web of uncertainty. You have your eye on a promising horse, but doubts creep in. Are you asking the right questions? Is there something missing? You don't want to make a costly mistake. This feeling of overwhelm is all too common.

Many buyers share this anxiety, fearing they might choose the wrong horse or miss crucial details.

Horse traders and dealers have not had a good reputation over the centuries, only replaced by the poor reputations of some used car salesmen!

However, with a bit of knowledge and some checklists to work through, you can be sensibly guided to finding the horse for your situation without putting yourself at risk or being taken for a ride.

Buy The Right Horse is designed to give you the essential steps to buying a horse, whether it be a pleasure riding horse, a competition horse, or a breeding horse. This book captures everything you need to know to ask the seller the right questions.

The purpose of this book is simple yet powerful. It is here to give you the tools and confidence you need to make wise decisions when buying a horse. Whether you are new to the process or have years of experience, this guide will empower you. With the proper knowledge, you can avoid pitfalls and find the horse that genuinely fits your needs.

***

Making memories – Image by Patrick Ryan, showing wonderful family horses.

Allow me to introduce myself. I am a passionate breeder with over 50 years of experience breeding, buying, and selling horses in South Australia. Throughout my career, I have learned valuable lessons, many through trial and error. I have shared my knowledge in books and articles and have taught adult equine studies for over 19 years.

I aim to help you learn from my experiences to make your journey smoother, less time-consuming, and more rewarding.

This book is for a diverse group of readers. Whether you are a leisure rider wanting a calm companion, a buyer looking to find a project horse to resell, a stud owner seeking a broodmare or stallion, or a goal-seeking competitive rider, this guide is designed for you. It addresses the specific challenges each of you might face and offers tailored advice to meet your unique goals.

What sets this book apart is its comprehensive nature. It includes checklists, and real-world success stories from buyers. These resources provide a well-rounded view of the horse-buying process. They ensure you are prepared for every stage, from initial research to final decision.

Readers can expect to learn how to spot red flags, ask the right questions, and confidently evaluate potential horses. You'll discover how to avoid hidden health and temperament issues. The book also covers what to do if you're buying sight unseen and whether a vet check is necessary.

We'll take a step-by-step approach. You'll start with preparation—understanding your goals and setting expectations. Then, I'll guide you through the search process, showing you how to research and choose the right avenues. Then we'll look at protecting your interests via market knowledge, negotiation, insurance and legal considerations. Finally, we'll cover the integration of your new horse into your life, ensuring a smooth transition.

I encourage you to embrace this journey with enthusiasm and confidence. You are about to make an important decision, one that will bring joy and fulfillment to your life. With the guidance found in these pages, buying a horse can be smarter, safer, and more rewarding. Let's begin this journey with the assurance that you will have the knowledge and tools to succeed.

Find the right horse for you here –your dream horse, unicorn, companion, best friend, or the one to build your stud.

If you like what you read, please tell your friends and leave a review on Amazon to help others find this book.

***

Chapter 1

How to buy a horse without the headaches

Know your 'why'

Congratulations!

You have come to the right place to learn about buying a horse. This information is based on my reflections on over 50+ years of breeding Australian Stock Horses in South Australia under the *Chalani* prefix. It comes from both a seller AND buyer perspective, over many years of buying horses for the stud and selling horses bred by us.

First things first

The first thing you need to do is be certain of the type of horse you are looking for. Before you do your research, decide what you need based on your experience (or lack thereof) and the things that will be deal-breakers for you.

There is no point asking or advertising for, say, a bay gelding 16 hands registered Quarter Horse around 10years old, suitable for hubby to ride if, instead, you'll settle for a 15h grey part-Arabian unregistered mare 4 years old, which your teen will ride and husband probably never. Don't laugh, it happens!

As these are quite different, you will give the seller the wrong idea completely or search pointlessly in the wrong places. Changing your mind mid-stream for something else that comes up is likely to result in you buying the wrong horse.

When it comes to horse ownership, what are you truly aiming for?

Whether you dream of leisurely riding through new scenery or envision the thrill of competitive showjumping, defining your ambitions is the most important first step.

A friend bought a horse recently. She imagined peaceful rides on quiet country paths but found herself with a reactive horse in company, and energy more suited for eventing than gentle strolls. This mismatch highlights the importance of aligning one's vision with the reality of your own experience. This is an all-too-common happening, and many can relate to this experience.

Remember, you are not looking for the perfect horse - you are looking for the perfect horse for you!

You will also need to know the level of quality you will be after, which will be dependent on what you want to do with the horse (such as show-ring or local riding club). Know what quality is by educating yourself or taking a mentor.

If you "don't care what it looks like," that is what you will likely get. A good horse doesn't need to be pretty, but he does need the basics of good structure and sound legs.

Define your ambitions

Start by considering what you hope to achieve with horse ownership. Are you seeking the pleasure of recreational riding, or are your eyes set on the show ring? Perhaps breeding appeals to you, or maybe you're looking for a quiet companion the family can ride. Defining these ambitions sets the foundation for making informed decisions.

A personal vision statement can guide you, reminding you of your ultimate goals. It provides clarity and direction, ensuring each choice aligns with your aspirations. Short-term goals, like mastering basic riding skills or attending local shows, should support longer-term ambitions such as competing at national levels or establishing a breeding program. This alignment ensures each step taken is purposeful and contributes to your broader vision.

The lifestyle you lead plays a significant role in shaping your horse ownership experience. Urban dwellers might face challenges such as limited space and access to riding areas, while rural residents often find more freedom in these aspects. Understanding your lifestyle's influence helps you make practical choices.

Commitment levels vary; you might have ample time for daily interaction and training while others juggle work, family, and equine pursuits. Space availability is another consideration. Do you have enough room at home for a stable and turnout, or will you need to find agistment? These factors impact the type of horse you might choose and the logistics of care and management.

Your current experience level with horses should heavily influence your choice. If you're inexperienced, having only ridden at riding schools, a horse known for its gentle nature might suit you best, offering a forgiving partner as you learn the ropes. More experienced riders can handle the challenges of a young horse or that of an off-the-track Thoroughbred, pushing their skills further. Among those looking to compete or tackle complex disciplines, advanced training is needed, so the horse matches in both temperament and capability.

It's important to recognize where you stand to avoid overreaching, which can be dangerous or, at the very least, frustrate both you and your horse.

Expectations must align with your practical realities, such as time, budget, and resources. In particular, whatever level you are at, you will also need to factor in lessons and clinics to enable you to grow, for you and your horse will require further education so as not to slip into bad habits.

You must ride many horses over time to learn about them, their nature, and their training. As you become more skilled, the first horse you bought may no longer be suitable for you to progress further. You may find yourself with new ambitions or outgrow the horse that started you off; a horse with more ability or education may be needed.

As I was learning, I would ride many people's horses to get the "feel" for them, their level of education, and their athletic abilities. As friends, we often swapped horses for a trail ride or went to the beach. It is important to recognise an uncomfortable truth—*that you cannot become a horseman riding only one horse.* This can come as a rude shock to the person buying their next horse, after having had the same horse for 20 years or so, giving them anxious thoughts about trying out new horses.

Your past experience will dictate the level of training you will need. Be truthful about this so you aren't presented with the wrong types of horses!

Another thing to consider is your price point and how flexible you are with this. You must be realistic about what your money can actually buy for you. If you have trouble finding something in your price range, you should reconsider if what you are looking for is realistic and change your expectations. Good horses *are* expensive, especially if you want one in the 7-15 year age range with a good deal of training under its belt.

Owning a horse is a significant commitment, demanding regular interaction, ongoing training, and a financial investment. Time investment involves daily routines such as travel, feeding, grooming, and exercise, which require dedication and consistency. Your life will revolve around these routines, which soon become chores if you don't love what you are doing.

Financial planning is equally vital; consider the initial purchase price and ongoing costs like feed, veterinary care, and equipment. Without careful planning, these expenses can quickly add up, leading to strain on your budget. Setting realistic expectations and aligning them with your resources will create a sustainable and fulfilling ownership experience.

Remember, if you have very set expectations, you can miss out on some horses that may be suitable. Using the above analogy, a Quarter Horse *mare* might fill the bill, but you have cut out half of your potential matches by insisting it be a gelding.

Matching horse type to your riding style

Understanding the distinct features of various horse types can greatly enhance your riding experience. Each discipline demands specific characteristics, and choosing the right horse can make all the difference. Consider dressage, where precision and grace are paramount. Horses bred for this discipline, like the Andalusian, Friesian, or Warmbloods, exhibit natural athleticism and a calm demeanor, essential for the intricate movements required. They possess an elegant carriage and a collected, rhythmic gait.

In contrast, trail riding necessitates endurance and a steady temperament. Breeds such as the Connemara, the Australian Stock Horse, or gaited breeds, known for their smooth gait and friendly nature, offer a comfortable ride over long distances and varied terrain. These horses provide the reliability and stamina needed for exploring outdoors, making them ideal companions for leisure riders.

Temperament is a critical factor in ensuring safety and enjoyment during rides. A calm horse offers a sense of security, especially for novice riders or those seeking tranquility. Calm breeds, like the Haflinger, Fjord, or Quarter Horse, are known for their easy-going nature and are often favored by families and recreational riders. On the other hand, sensitive horses such as the Thoroughbred or Arabian bring energy, appealing to experienced riders who enjoy the challenge of bringing on a competitive mount.

Matching a horse's temperament with the rider's style is crucial. A mismatch can lead to tension or even accidents, as a high-energy horse paired with an over-confident rider might become unpredictable; even a quiet horse with a nervous beginner can soon test a rider who doesn't notice the early signs of bad manners.

Assessing temperament involves observing a horse's behavior in various situations. Does it spook easily, or does it remain composed in new environments? These observations provide valuable insights into a horse's suitability for your needs.

Physical attributes also play a significant role in determining a horse's suitability for specific riding styles. Conformation, or the shape and structure of a horse, affects its movement and performance. Dressage horses require exceptional balance and a strong top line to execute movements with precision and fluidity. Structural correctness ensures soundness and reduces the risk of injury, especially in disciplines demanding agility and coordination. For endurance riding, stamina is paramount. Such a horse may not be suitable for weekend riding. An endurance horse must withstand long hours without fatigue, maintaining its pace and stability over sometimes rough terrain.

The truth about horse buying

Evaluating these attributes for the various disciplines requires a keen eye, often involving a thorough analysis of the horse's build and quality of movement. In these instances, it is best to have a person experienced in the discipline and with knowledge of your riding abilities to advise you throughout the process.

Novice riders benefit from forgiving and tolerant horses, allowing them to build confidence gradually. Breeds like the Morgan Horse or Welsh cob, known for their versatility and friendly nature, offer a supportive partnership for those still honing their skills. As skills develop, more experienced riders might seek horses that challenge them, pushing their abilities further. Balancing challenge with safety is key; a horse that is too advanced may overwhelm a rider, while one that is too stoic might hinder progress.

To understand a horse's temperament, observe its interactions with people and other horses. Notice its responses to sudden noises or unfamiliar objects. Is it curious, cautious, or indifferent?

These reactions reveal how a horse might behave in various situations. Conduct a simple test by leading the horse in different environments, noting any signs of anxiety or calmness. Such exercises help you gauge a horse's temperament and readiness for your chosen discipline.

It's about finding a partner that complements your current skills while encouraging growth. This balance ensures both horse and rider succeed and enjoy their time together.

Even if you are after a broodmare or a young, unbroken horse, you need to be thorough in your questions – find out the broodmare's history or that of the parents of the foal so you can make an appropriate assessment as to suitability.

Young or unbroken horses are not suitable for beginners or novices.

Don't be fooled into thinking that a well-trained horse will suit you just because it appears quiet. It may be too sensitive, too quick in its movements, or only that way when ridden by a pro. Don't be fooled into thinking that a relaxed and friendly horse is automatically a quiet horse to ride.

Start your search far and wide before you are ready to buy to assess the market and learn what is likely to come up in your price range. This is important – if you do not know, you will be less likely to trust your judgment when the right horse becomes available. Instead, you will likely procrastinate and lose out on the purchase because the seller has taken another offer.

***

Chapter 2

Understanding the types of horses to buy

What is the right type for you?

L et's look at the types of horses out there and the different reasons for buying them.

Schoolmasters

In the equestrian world, a schoolmaster is a term revered by many for good reason. These horses are not just about their ability to perform; they are the patient teachers of the horse world. A good schoolmaster is defined by its experience, patience, and temperament. Experience speaks to the horse's history—years of work under saddle, exposure to various environments, and the challenges it has faced and overcome.

This wealth of experience translates into a calm confidence, essential for guiding less experienced riders. Patience is another pillar. Schoolmasters possess the rare ability to tolerate their riders' mistakes. They remain steady even when commands are unclear or when a rider is learning to balance and move in harmony with their horse.

Temperament is equally important, as it defines the horse's ability to remain calm in diverse situations, providing a safe learning environment. These traits combined create an ideal partner for anyone looking to develop their riding skills, and choosing a horse with these attributes can significantly enrich your learning experience and make a wonderful friend.

The role of a schoolmaster in skill development cannot be overstated. These horses serve as a stable foundation for learning, providing you with a consistent and reliable platform on which to build your skills.

Unlike a younger, less experienced horse, a schoolmaster can offer immediate feedback by helping riders understand the nuances of balance, rhythm, and communication. When a rider makes an error, a schoolmaster often compensates, allowing the rider to correct himself without the fear of losing control.

This environment fosters confidence, as riders feel secure knowing their horse can handle unexpected situations. Teaching opportunities abound with a schoolmaster as they introduce riders to more complex maneuvers and techniques, gradually increasing difficulty as the rider's competence grows.

This structured approach to learning ensures that the rider progresses steadily, building a solid foundation for future growth and challenges.

Evaluating potential schoolmasters requires a keen eye and understanding of specific traits and behaviors. Consistency in performance is paramount; a schoolmaster should demonstrate reliability across various scenarios, from the quiet of a home arena to the hustle and bustle of a showground.

Adaptability to rider errors is an important trait. A true schoolmaster will remain composed when a rider makes a mistake, offering the opportunity to learn and adjust without causing unnecessary stress. For this reason, they are in high demand and are usually expensive.

Evaluating these horses should involve observing them in different environments and noting their responses to new and potentially stressful situations. Watch them in the sport they're currently competing in. Are they calm and focused, or do they become anxious? A checklist of these traits can guide you in making an informed decision, ensuring your chosen horse will serve as a true partner.

Realize that even after purchasing a schoolmaster, the learning process continues. That is the purpose of buying a schoolmaster!

Post-purchase support is vital to maximizing the benefits of owning such a horse. Spend the time to work with the previous owner to learn the horse's aids. Often schoolmaster horses mentally struggle and shut down when the new owner uses totally different buttons. The owner becomes disappointed with the horse. So guidance from an experienced instructor provides invaluable assistance, helping you fully understand and utilize your horse's capabilities.

They can offer tailored exercises that build towards your goals, ensuring you grow as a partnership together and keep both you and your horse engaged and challenged. This ongoing development helps maintain the horse's physical and mental health while also enhancing your skills and confidence. Involving others in your equestrian journey enriches your experience and ensures you are supported every step of the way.

Safe ponies for children

When selecting a pony for a child, safety is paramount. They are the "schoolmaster" for children. A pony's demeanor must be calm, as an excitable or unpredictable temperament can quickly turn what should be a joyful experience into a daunting one.

A pony with a gentle disposition acts as a steadfast partner, encouraging a child to build confidence in their riding abilities. Their calm nature ensures that even if the child makes a mistake, the pony remains unflustered, providing a stable platform for learning.

Predictable behavior is necessary. A pony that responds consistently to commands and stimuli allows a child to anticipate and understand its actions, which is essential for developing riding skills. This predictability helps the child learn to communicate effectively with the pony, fostering a sense of security and trust.

Size is another vital consideration when choosing a pony for young riders. Child-appropriate size means that the pony should be proportionate to the child's stature, ensuring the rider can mount, dismount, and ride comfortably without assistance.

It should be a size that, with time, the child can learn to saddle and bridle himself. A pony that is too large can intimidate a child, while one that is too small may not provide the necessary stability for learning. And the child will grow out of it too soon. The ideal size allows the child to feel in control, promoting independence and confidence in handling the pony.

Additionally, the pony's training level plays a significant role in safety. A well-trained pony easily responds to beginner-friendly commands, offering a straightforward and uncomplicated riding experience.

Such training includes being accustomed to the lead rein and lunging, which is often used during initial lessons to guide the pony while the child learns the basics of riding. This familiarity with lead rein work provides an added layer of safety, ensuring the pony remains calm and responsive under the guidance of an adult or instructor. It also provides a means to lead the pony from another horse, so parent and child can ride out on the trail, for added interest and enjoyment.

While a sound pony is essential for ride-outs with another horse, an older, slightly arthritic, or previously laminitic pony, may be suitable for a year or so for a complete child beginner if under medical supervision. Don't dismiss an older, healthy horse, even one in its 20s, as many of these can be extremely safe and sound for the purpose. But you will need to consider the extra commitment of feeding and medical costs in retirement and probable euthanasia down the track.

Many good ponies can be found by asking around at your local pony club for a pony that will be moved on from its current family. Such ponies may only be available on lease, as the family wants to ensure a good home. Check out the conditions, if so, as these are sometimes the best option. They can provide a

The child's pony should be selected for temperament, soundness and versatility, to build the child's confidence and abilities. Xander Ide with Tooravale Indiana.

stop-gap measure until the rider has more experience, and you have the knowledge you can return the pony if it doesn't work out, or when the child grows out of it, which it inevitably will.

Supervision is essential, especially in the early stages of learning, as it helps integrate safety practices seamlessly into the child's riding routine. Adults can ensure safety by insisting on the use of appropriate gear. Safety gear, such as helmets, good-quality riding boots, protective vests, and properly fitted saddles and bridles, should always be worn, as a barrier against potential injury.

Continuous involvement from a knowledgeable adult ensures that the child is riding safely and learns proper techniques from the start. Supervised riding sessions allow for immediate correction of mistakes, preventing the formation of bad habits and ensuring that the child understands the reasons behind each correction.

If you are looking for a show pony or a child's hunter, this is a very specialized area, and the sky's the limit for pricing. Shetlands, Riding Ponies, Australian Ponies, and the Welsh Pony (A& B) are the usual breeds of choice. Unless you are an experienced horse family, leave this to the professionals to find the right one for you after the child has developed a good seat and quiet hands.

Adult supervision and guidance are indispensable in a child's riding life and should always be factored in before buying a pony. After all, the question you need to ask yourself is, *"How much do I value my child's safety?"*

Choosing the right pony goes beyond simply picking one that looks appealing. It involves carefully evaluating temperament, size, and training to ensure that the pony meets the specific needs of a young rider.

An older pony is perfect for the beginner child rider. They can be absolute gems. A safe pony encourages, supports, and nurtures a child's budding interest in riding, laying the groundwork for a lifelong passion.

Checklist for choosing a child's pony:

- Have you vetted potential ponies through trustworthy recommendations?

- Do you have a support network (instructors, fellow pony parents) to guide you?

- Does the pony have a gentle, calm demeanor?

- Is the pony predictable in its reactions to noise, movement, or new environments?

- Will the pony tolerate beginner mistakes without spooking?

- Does the pony respect boundaries without pulling on the lead or grabbing grass at every opportunity?

- Can your child mount and dismount independently?

- Is the pony small enough to manage yet big enough to offer stability?

- Will the pony's size allow your child to gradually learn to saddle and bridle on their own?

- Is the pony well-versed in lead rein and lunging?

- Can the pony walk, trot, and stop smoothly on cue?

- Does the pony respond well to basic, gentle commands?

- Has the pony been exposed to trails, roads, or other environments similar to where your child will ride?

- Does the pony remain calm under a child's handling?

- Will it tolerate grooming, tacking, and leading from a child?

- Is the pony comfortable on it's own and in company with other horses, or does it become insecure without it's paddock buddy being close by?

- Is there a plan for adult supervision during all rides?

- Does your child have proper safety gear—helmet, boots, vest?

- Is the pony sound for regular, light riding? (Has the pony been cleared by a vet?)

- Does the pony have health concerns or manageable conditions like arthritis?

- Are you ready to commit to the care and costs of a pony once its riding days are over, including euthanasia?

The learner's horse

This is basically a repeat of the purchase process for a child rider, with the exception that you will be looking for a horse for an adult. Therefore, you need to consider the height of the horse and your weight to make a suitable size match. Horses that are not too tall and have some breadth offer a feeling of security for learner adults. Suitable breeds are a "been there, done that" Quarter Horse or Cob type, or even a part Clydesdale for the taller, heavier rider.

Check how easily it travels on a long rein and if it can walk out well in company without getting excited. How easily will it stop on request? As they say, you want something with "more whoa than go." The more nervous the rider, the more stoic the horse must be. A horse over the age of 15 is likely set in its ways, so if it is reliable now, it will likely stay that way.

Don't make the mistake that you consider yourself no longer a beginner just because you have been to a few trail rides and camps or lessons at a local riding school. You won't have much foundational knowledge, and you certainly won't have the experience your new horse will have had. And he will soon realize that and test you out. This can come as a rude shock for a learner. So he will need to be forgiving, gentle, and very calm-natured, as well as experienced in many situations.

Look for a horse which you can take full responsibility for both its care needs and riding. Find one that has served a family well for some years, and they will be the best at advising you on how to progress with the horse. If it is your first horse, how does it behave without the company of other horses? Can you have riding lessons at your place, or do you need to travel a distance with your horse for ride-outs, instruction, and clinics? How would you handle an emergency if you needed to take a colicky horse to your veterinary clinic?

Can you do this all on your own, or can you enlist a helper at short notice?

Answering these questions should tell you if you are ready to buy your first horse or wait until you have had more lessons and experience.

The leisure horse

Many recreational riders are prepared to pay more money for a horse which will last them into retirement, and though they don't intend to compete, (local fun days excepted) they may have demands for fitness and training levels of the horse they are looking for.

The recreational rider likes to do clinics, beach rides, liberty work, trail rides and long distance treks, overnight camping, musical rides, cushion polo, ranch riding, Riding Club, military and medieval re-enactments, and parades – The list can go on!

If your plans for the next few years are to use your horse for recreational riding only, you need to understand the basic guidelines for the child's pony and beginner's horse and establish in your mind where you sit in regards to your riding experience and training goals. You might be looking for a younger horse between the ages of 7-15 years, that can satisfy your requirements, which is the horse's prime years. This will have him cost much more!

You need a horse with a background in many experiences, so take your time. These horses are in huge demand, so be prepared to pay almost as much as a competition horse for the right one. You will also need to keep him and yourself "tuned," so factor in the costs of taking yourself to instructional days, so you don't go backwards and can learn new skills.

The competition horse

Competition horses are always in high demand, and prices reflect this, depending on the discipline involved. Going horses with a proven track record in competition, sound and well placed to move into elite levels are priced out of reach of most people and are often out of reach to insure them.

Most professional riders cannot fund their top competition horses without extra funding from sponsorships or benevolent (or paying) owners. Others buy young horses and commit to training them up to the levels they wish to compete. This may even be the case with a medium-level horse, one with the ability to move on up the levels but with sufficiently trustworthy foundation to advance a rider's progress.

Performance history also significantly influences value. A horse with a track record of competition success or consistent performance on the field assures buyers of its reliability and skill. Age, too, plays a role. While younger horses may promise longevity and potential, older horses with proven records offer immediate usefulness and command top dollar. A few quirky behaviours may be tolerated, but the horse must demonstrate genuine ability and heart. You want to be capable enough to ride it into the winner's circle yourself.

What fun is horse ownership if you buy a horse that only a pro can ride and you step on it at the last minute to go into the ring?

You must thoroughly research your chosen sport well before you intend to purchase. Write a list of your "must haves" and non-negotiables. Put your name down at suitable establishments so that you might be advised of a private sale before the horse is advertised. Help out at show stables and hunter/jumper establishments, or become a polo groom or strapper to develop your abilities and show commitment.

Check out breed papers, vaccinations, health certificates, genetic testing, history, x-ray reports, current insurance, and the like if a horse interests you. Be prepared to fly out at short notice to inspect the horse of your choice and take your instructor with you if necessary.

Beware: There are so many medium and top-level horses with soundness issues, on medications to keep them sound, and traumatized by unethical training practices that you will need to double down on your research as to who you can trust. You still want a sound horse that you can enjoy. Also make sure it is good to float.

From observation a huge moving Warmblood is not for your average rider if you are looking for a competition dressage horse. You have to be extremely athletic and fit to sit and go with this huge stride/movement. What very often happens is they are bought by amateur riders who end up sending them to professional riders to school because they can't sit the movement, or as a consequence, the owner ends up shutting down the movement so they can ride it.

This is so detrimental to the horse. Either they end up losing their quality of movement or worse become bio-mechanically and mentally unsound. If you are older and not as physically fit as you once were competing in your youth, buy an average/smaller moving Warmblood with movement you can sit to and enjoy .

So buy what you can ride, bearing in mind your age, fitness, health and abilities.

In most cases you will want a registered horse. This is because of the value you are placing on it. A registered horse also usually means you have access to special end of year breed awards, and other benefits which either give you discounts, or added prizemoney, when a horse of your breed does well in open competition. It also gives you access to your breed's exclusive shows and competitions, which a non-registered horse is ineligible for. It opens the door for more activities and training clinics by elite trainers which are often hard to access otherwise. A registered horse is usually easier to sell later if you need to.

When viewing a competition horse, make sure you see it demonstrating the types of activities it is trained in. Evaluate your own skills and fitness levels accordingly. Kim Ide with Chalani Card Tricks. PYT photography.

The all-rounder

These are versatile horses of a steady temperament, for a teenager, or amateur rider who likes to try their skills at many types of events. Stepping up from a pony can be a big ask for some teenagers. Perhaps they are not sure what discipline they like the best; though they may have an interest in showjumping, they'd like an attractive horse they can take into the show ring with some success, and perhaps do some cross country eventing, which will require a horse that can do a reasonable dressage test. The teenager is keen to ride every day after school and spends most of her time with her horse, practicing obstacles, jumping or riding on the beach. It must be good to float.

This horse needs to be cool minded, athletic and willing to have a go at anything it is tried at, with the movement and elegance for the show ring. It is probably between the age of 5-12 years, with enough education for the horse to do a reliable dressage test. It may be a bit quirky, but nothing a keen teenager can't handle. Indeed a little quirkiness may be a reason they bond together so well forming a long term partnership. Teenagers love their horse's personality and uniqueness. This horse takes the teenager from a keen rider to an accomplished rider in several disciplines, often giving her results far beyond what she thought possible.

A true all-rounder will have shown it can handle a wide variety of events, or otherwise have the potential and education for such.

The project horse

Horses, like any other valuable asset, have the potential for reselling. This concept centers around the idea that, with the right choice, a horse can appreciate in value over time.

If you are looking for a project, consider an unbroken young horse to bring on and train for resale. Or you might buy one cheaply because it requires rehabilitation or retraining.

Or consider a horse to which you can give extensive training, developing skills in a discipline that make it highly desirable to potential buyers of that discipline. A ready-to-compete competition horse is in huge demand and can command a good price (see p 14).

Such a horse offers immediate enjoyment and serves as a potential source of profit if sold later. The investment increases when the horse successfully competes, earning awards that boost its market appeal.

Evaluating a horse's resale potential involves several critical factors. Pedigree, quality, and athleticism are primary considerations.

Horses with generations of champions or notable sires and dams close in their pedigree generally command higher prices. This background informs you about the horse's potential capabilities and attributes.

Market demand trends fluctuate, influenced by changing discipline preferences or breeding standards. Staying informed about these shifts can help you anticipate future value changes and make strategic buying decisions.

However, buying a project horse involves risks, and managing these is essential. Injury is a primary concern, as a seemingly minor issue can drastically affect a horse's value and utility. A thorough health assessment by a qualified veterinarian can identify possible problems, allowing you to make informed decisions.

Insurance offers another layer of protection, covering unexpected health issues, accidents, or loss. Policies tailored to equestrian needs can safeguard your investment, ensuring peace of mind in the face of uncertainties.

Strategic buying involves selecting horses with clear growth potential, whether through training, breeding, or competition. In my experience, buying a half-started or half-finished project horse needs the potential to double your money, or it is not worth the purchase.

You can look at it another way: The project buyer wants at least $5k on top of their purchase price just to recoup their own costs, plus extra for the time and training put into it. Therefore, if you are selling it for $10K, you don't want to spend more than $3k on a purchase. Plenty of project buyers start small and progress by buying horses in higher price brackets as they sell one to fund the next.

Elite traders have an attitude that any horse they own has a price on its head. They may also train horses on commission as agents so that you might find your next horse through them.

Some project buyers have the eye to buy horses that others see little merit in and can turn them over into worthy animals in short periods of time. Smart buyers have even been known to buy an unkempt horse in the morning at auction and wash, clip, and polish it up for resale later in the day for a tidy profit!

The freebie

Sometimes, you may be offered a horse for no cost, where a good home is the only concern. But as they say, don't look a gift horse in the mouth. It might be much older than you think! If it has been spelling in a paddock for 5 years and not ridden since it was broken in, that is a red flag. Ensure you get a history of the horse and full disclosure of its past health before agreeing to such a proposal. If you take the horse, pay $1 for it and get a receipt. Otherwise you run the risk of the owner wanting it back sometime later, after he sees you are successful with it, claiming it was only a loan.

The rescue horse

Such horses are usually found at a sanctuary or shelter to rehabilitate neglected or surrendered animals. These horses are often weak, aged, unsound, traumatized, and needing medical care. Adoption fees apply, and you will be vetted for suitability and given a history of the horse. Most of the horses found here will only be suitable as companions or with limits to their riding usage, so I cannot make any recommendation for finding a horse through these services.

The young horse

This horse is most likely found at the home of the breeder. It could be a weanling or something up to breaking age. A buyer with some training experience will often buy a young horse to develop himself simply because he is frustrated with buying other people's problems in the past and no longer wants the hassle.

It may well be the first time he has broken a horse in, and he wants to learn the process. He wants to start on something with a clean slate.

It is often an opportunity to buy a higher quality horse than you could afford if it was much older. You are buying it on its potential, not what it has proven to have done. A highly trained competitive horse may well be out of most people's reach.

In this situation it is important to either see the parents, or at least research the parents, to have an understanding of their respective temperaments, and the usual disciplines and prices they go for.

Does it have straight legs and a correct structure? Does it move straight? Does it look like either of the parents? What height will it grow to?

Some foals look beautiful as babies but plain off as they grow; others may be awkward, leggy, ugly ducklings with the potential to turn into beautiful swans. Most young horses will be"bum-high" until they mature, but make sure this is not excessive, or they will never grow out of it. Check the parents and siblings for similar characteristics.

Does the chosen young horse live up to expectations when you view it? Is it friendly out in the paddock? What handling has it already had? Can this be demonstrated by observing it or watching a video? What are its older siblings doing?

These are questions you may not have answers for, so to some extent, you must rely on the responses from the breeder. Therefore, you must find a breeder who, by reputation, is trustworthy; perhaps an old-timer who knows the industry inside and out, who can point you in the right direction. If you are purchasing a young horse, you need to consider its socialization with other horses, its growing needs, and the long-term nature of the purchase. Can you take it out and about for experience? Will you have the time, energy, and sufficient expertise to put into it?

There is no point buying something "so you can grow together" if, in four years, you have still not been able to give it the training it needs to become quiet and easily handled. Horses are expensive pasture ornaments!

There is nothing more rewarding than starting a young horse from scratch, knowing you have developed it yourself.

Chapter 3

Preparing for your search

Essential checklists for success

A well-crafted checklist becomes your compass, guiding you through the myriad of choices and ensuring you stay focused on what truly matters. A checklist is your anchor.

It transforms the complex process of horse buying into a structured, manageable task, allowing you to approach each decision with clarity and confidence.

Crafting a comprehensive horse-buying checklist begins with understanding the essential components that must be included. Health and veterinary records are paramount, offering insights into the horse's current health status, past medical issues, and vaccination records. These documents reveal potential hidden health problems that could impact the horse's long-term well-being.

Equally important is the training and performance history, which provides a snapshot of the horse's capabilities and achievements. Whether you're assessing a schoolmaster's experience or a young horse's potential, this history helps you gauge suitability for your specific goals.

Temperament assessment criteria should also feature prominently. Observations of how a horse interacts with humans and other horses give you a sense of its personality, behavior, manners, and training.

Your checklist should reflect your personal riding goals and lifestyle. For instance, if you're a leisure rider, prioritize traits such as calmness and ease of handling. Stud breeders focus on pedigree, absence of genetic disorders, conformation, and breeding potential. Lifestyle factors, such as the amount of time you can dedicate to training and care, must be considered. Tailoring the checklist to your unique circumstances ensures it remains a valuable tool rather than a generic list of attributes.

This personalized approach helps you stay aligned with your vision, making it easier to identify horses that truly fit your requirements.

Organization and planning cannot be overstated in the buying process. A well-organized checklist prevents oversight and ensures a thorough evaluation of each horse.

Prioritizing your needs is vital. Identify which traits are non-negotiable and which can be flexible. This clarity helps streamline your selection process, focusing your efforts on horses that meet your essential criteria while allowing room for compromise.

Approach your search step-by step, from initial enquiries to final decision, using your checklist to guide each stage.

Maintaining this structured approach minimizes the risk of impulsive decisions that could lead to regret or financial loss.

As you gain more insight and experience, revise and update your checklist. Feedback is a powerful tool; learn from each enquiry and past purchases, noting what worked and what didn't. Refine your criteria, ensuring your checklist evolves with your growing expertise. Learning from past purchases equips you with a deeper understanding of your true needs and preferences, allowing you to make more informed decisions.

Regularly revisit and adjust your checklist. Keep it relevant and effective, ensuring it continues to serve as a reliable guide in your horse-buying endeavors.

Step 1: Personal checklist: lifestyle considerations

Before you start horse shopping, take a step back and think about how a new horse will fit into your lifestyle, time commitments, skills, fitness and budget. Owning a horse is a long-term responsibility, so make sure the decision aligns with your goals and circumstances. Here's a personal checklist to guide you:

Define your non-negotiables

What are the **top three traits** your new horse must have? These should be based on your specific riding goals, experience level, and lifestyle.

Examples:

- Safe and reliable for a beginner rider.

- Sound and healthy, with no history of lameness.

- Calm temperament, suitable for trail riding, willingness to go over obstacles.

Your non-negotiables:

-

-

Assess your riding goals and needs

Think about your **short-term and long-term goals** with this horse. Do you want a competition horse, a trail buddy, or a future broodmare? Your checklist should reflect these needs.

Questions to ask yourself:

- What discipline or activity will I focus on (dressage, jumping, trail riding, working equitation)?

- Do I need a horse with specific training or one I can train myself?

- Am I looking for one with potential or an older, experienced horse?

- What health considerations are non-negotiable (e.g. no history of lameness, clean vet records)?

Your Notes:

-

-

Evaluate your lifestyle

Owning a horse is a **time-intensive** commitment. Make sure you can balance horse ownership with your other responsibilities.

Lifestyle considerations:

- How much time can I dedicate to riding, training, and care each week?

- Do I have suitable facilities (e.g. stable, paddock, access to trails)?

- Am I prepared to handle seasonal care changes (rugging, feed adjustments)?

- What support network do I have (trainer, farrier, vet, friends to help)?

-

Assess your lifestyle compatibility

Ensure that owning a horse fits into your **daily life and future plans**.

Questions to ask yourself:

- Do I have enough time to commit to a horse every day?

- What will I do if my circumstances change (job, health, family)?

- How far am I willing to travel to care for or ride the horse?

- Do I have a backup plan for holidays or emergencies?

-

-

Build and refine your checklist

Use this checklist as a starting point. With every horse you view, update your notes and refine your criteria based on what works and what doesn't.

Example:

- After viewing a few horses, you may realize you prioritize ground manners more than competition experience.

- Or you may decide you need a horse with a quiet temperament, even if it means compromising on breed or color – you may decide that your dream breed doesn't match your skill-set or fitness levels.

Remember:

- Stay realistic about your needs.

- Don't compromise on safety or soundness.

- Learn from each viewing to make your checklist more accurate.

"The right horse isn't always the flashiest or the cheapest—it's the one that fits your lifestyle and goals best."

Step 2: Access local networks, resources, and information

Understanding the local equestrian landscape is essential for making informed decisions. Local events and networks provide a wealth of information and opportunities to connect with other horse enthusiasts. Attending these events allows you to ask about horses available for sale, observe horses in action, assess potential purchases, and gather insights from seasoned riders and breeders.

The connections made here can lead to valuable advice and even future partnerships.

Regional equestrian associations are an excellent resource, offering a platform to meet professionals who can guide your buying process. Find out what associations are strong in your area. These associations often host clinics, workshops, and networking events, providing further opportunities to deepen your understanding and make informed choices. Establishing relationships with these experts can provide ongoing support and ensure you have access to the best knowledge and resources available.

Finding region-specific horse listings involves tapping into the right resources. Local classifieds and online groups are a great starting point, often featuring horses available nearby. These platforms allow you to connect directly with sellers, ask questions, and arrange visits.

Regional horse shows also present opportunities to find horses suited to your needs. These events showcase various breeds and disciplines, giving you the chance to see horses perform and interact with others. Attending these shows helps you find potential purchases and provides a deeper understanding of the local market.

To do:

- Add the names and contacts of people you have talked to, as well as the topic or the name of the organization, to your email list of Contacts.

- Keep business cards of tradespeople and professionals.

- Record notes detailing any conversations.

Step 3: Find a mentor

This may be the most important step in the whole process. The guidance of local experts and mentors can offer tailored advice based on regional conditions. Local trainers and riding instructors possess invaluable knowledge about your area's specific challenges and opportunities. They can provide insights into which breeds and temperaments work best locally, and they may even know of horses for sale that suit your needs.

Establish a rapport with someone whose opinion you respect and who will be prepared to guide you, even if it requires a fee. Work through the process of establishing your checklists with this person.

Remember, patience and persistence are key.

Step 4: Research market trends and pricing

Economic factors cast a wide net over the equestrian market, significantly influencing horse prices. During economic downturns, discretionary spending often decreases, affecting the demand for horses and potentially leading to lower prices.

Conversely, periods of economic growth can increase disposable income, boosting demand and driving prices up. The expansion of the equestrian market, now valued at around $300 billion globally, reflects this dynamic. The impact of the Olympic games every four years inspires competitors who dream of competing with a horse in those disciplines. Growth brings innovation and more participants, but it can also lead to increased competition and higher prices for sought-after breeds and abilities.

Venturing into the horse market without understanding its dynamics is like setting sail without a compass. Market trends dictate both the pricing and availability of horses and staying informed is your best ally. Your mentor will have in-depth knowledge and can guide you through this. Some regions are almost exclusively dominated by Western events, others by English, or a mix of the two. You may also find greater emphasis on some disciplines, such as eventing, polocrosse, or cutting.

Consider the current demand for specific breeds. For instance, a surge in interest in Gypsy horses due to their striking appearance and versatility may drive prices higher. More numerous breeds may be more affordable. These fluctuations are often influenced by trends in equestrian sports, changes in breeding practices, or even popular culture, where a horse featured in a movie or series can suddenly rise in demand.

Seasonal price fluctuations also play a role. Spring and summer, prime seasons for ridden activity and competitions, often see a spike in horse buying activity, leading to increased prices. Understanding these patterns lets you time your purchase strategically, potentially saving you money or securing a better deal.

Compare prices online or in breed magazine classifieds. Check the range of prices for similar horses across different regions. These platforms often provide filters for breed, age, and training level, giving you a clearer picture of what you might expect to pay.

Historical price data analysis can further enhance your understanding. By examining past trends, you can identify cycles and predict future shifts, helping you anticipate when prices might drop or rise. This proactive approach ensures you can make informed decisions aligning with your budget and goals.

Subscribe to equestrian magazines to keep yourself informed about market trends, new technologies, and shifts in consumer behavior, which is especially valuable if you are a breeder or competitor. Following breeders or industry leaders on social media offers another valuable resource. These people often share current updates and personal insights, giving you access to a community of like-minded individuals and the latest information.

Step 5: Utilizing online platforms for market research

In today's digital age, horse-buying has expanded far beyond traditional methods. With the rise of online platforms for equine sales, buyers have access to a wide array of websites and apps designed to facilitate horse purchases.

Equine classifieds websites have become go-to resources for many, offering detailed search filters that allow you to narrow down options by breed, location, and price range. These platforms provide an extensive selection, catering to diverse needs, whether you're a stud owner looking for a broodmare or a leisure rider seeking a trail companion.

Social media marketplaces, such as Facebook groups dedicated to horse sales, are extremely valuable. We sell most of our horses now by enquiries through Facebook and to a lesser extent, our website. Social media connects buyers directly with sellers, fostering a community where enthusiasts can share insights and opportunities.

The benefits of using online platforms for research are numerous. The digital realm offers a broader selection than what might be available locally, giving you access to horses from different regions and even countries. This variety increases the likelihood of finding a horse that perfectly matches your needs. Online listings often include user reviews and seller ratings, offering insights into previous buyers' experiences. These reviews help gauge a seller's reputation and the quality of their horses.

Access to such a wealth of information allows you to make informed decisions, reducing the risks of purchasing a horse. You can compare prices, pedigrees, and training levels across multiple listings.

Evaluating online listings requires a discerning eye. Start by analyzing photos and videos. High-quality visuals can reveal much about a horse's condition, conformation, and movement. Look for clear, well-lit images that show the horse from various angles, both standing and in motion. Videos should display the horse in different gaits and environments. Pay attention to the setting; a professional-looking environment might indicate serious sellers, while cluttered or low-quality imagery could raise red flags.

Communication patterns with the seller are equally telling. A responsive and transparent seller who provides detailed answers to your questions and willingly shares additional photos or videos is often more trustworthy. Be wary of those who evade queries or offer vague responses, as these could signal issues with the horse or the seller's credibility.

Step 6: Establishing a budget for your purchase

Embarking on the journey of buying a horse without a well-planned budget is akin to navigating unknown waters without a map. Establishing a realistic budget is crucial to avoid overspending and ensure you can comfortably manage *both the initial purchase and the ongoing costs of horse ownership.*

Prioritize your must-haves. Determine what attributes are non-negotiable for your needs, be it temperament, training level, or health, and focus your budget on these areas. You may need to compromise on age, height, sex, or breed so as not to compromise on other features. Being clear about what you can compromise on and what is essential will help streamline your choices, without stretching your finances beyond your means.

The initial purchase price is just one piece of the financial puzzle; long-term expenses can add up quickly. These include regular veterinary visits as required, transport costs if you're moving the horse from a distant location, and any initial equipment you may need. Budgeting for additional costs is vital. Horses can encounter health issues unexpectedly, and having a financial cushion for vet checks and treatment can prevent financial strain. Don't for get the old saying:

"Quality is remembered long after the price is forgotten."

Owning a horse is a long-term commitment that comes with various ongoing costs. Feed and care expenses form a substantial part of this commitment. Horses require a balanced diet, regular grooming, and periodic health checks to remain in top condition. Training and agistment fees are also significant considerations, particularly if you don't have the facilities to house and train the horse yourself.

Agistment fees vary widely depending on location and the level of care provided, ranging from basic pasture agistment to full-service stabling and turnout. Check what is available in your area, visit your best choices to see what is being offered, prices for each service, and when your horse can move in.

Read the contracts for each option and compare services with other places. Do you want budget-friendly where you do everything yourself, a close location, pasture feeding, riding facilities or trails nearby, or full livery? Is there an instructor on site, or who regularly visits? What about farriery services? Does the farrier visit regularly, or must you arrange it yourself? You will likely find a great range of options between facilities, so prepare well in advance of buying the horse as to what your needs are.

Breaking-in and training costs can also fluctuate based on the discipline and expertise of the trainer. It's important to factor these costs into your budget to ensure that you can provide a consistent and supportive environment for your horse.

Sometimes advertisements state "firm," o.n.o. (or near offer), "price negotiable" or "best price." Others may state "home more important than price" or "upon inquiry." Having the cash up front is a bargaining chip. Don't be afraid to negotiate a price or ask for additional inclusions, such as tack or transport assistance.

Successful negotiation hinges on several key elements, each playing a role in crafting a favorable outcome. Begin by understanding the seller's motivations. Are they looking to sell quickly due to personal circumstances, or are they seeking a specific price due to the horse's pedigree or training? This insight can inform your strategy, allowing you to tailor your approach to meet both parties' needs. Having these firmly in mind ensures you remain focused and don't get swept up in the emotion of the moment.

Communicate clearly. Articulate your needs and concerns confidently, ensuring the seller understands where you stand and what you expect.

Establishing a positive relationship with the seller fosters goodwill, making him more inclined to accommodate your requests. Perhaps you can use your past experience to highlight what you intend to do in the future with the horse. Perhaps you both value maintaining a good reputation within the equestrian community through promotional opportunities. Perhaps you will be invested in spreading the good word to others looking to buy.

While it's important to advocate for your needs, being overly aggressive or inflexible can alienate the seller, closing off potential avenues for compromise. Balance is key. Present your terms firmly but respectfully, allowing room for dialogue and adjustment.

Exploring financing options can provide the flexibility to acquire a horse without immediate financial strain. Some sellers offer payment plans, allowing you to spread the cost over a period of time before delivery. But don't *expect* a seller to provide you with terms. If you must, get a loan to pay him **in full**. Arrange your finances in advance so you can pay up front at the time of purchase.

Approaching sellers with a clear understanding of the market and the horse's value can lead to more favorable terms.

Flexible arrangements can be particularly beneficial if you're purchasing a high-value horse and need to manage cash flow.

Equestrian loan programs and sponsorships are another option, providing funds specifically for horse purchases. These typically have terms that reflect the unique nature of equestrian activities, though not necessarily offering competitive interest rates or flexible repayment schedules, compared with going to your own bank. It's essential to research these options thoroughly and understand the terms and conditions to avoid unexpected costs or commitments. Such terms often mandate insurance to protect your investment, which in itself can be quite expensive.

Balancing quality and cost is a delicate act, but getting the best value for your budget is possible without compromising on quality.

Finally, ensure that your financial transactions are conducted through secure payment methods. Being vigilant and cautious helps safeguard you and ensures that your buying experience is both safe and successful. This diligence mirrors the careful preparation and research that is critical in every aspect of horse buying.

Online security is paramount when engaging in digital horse-buying transactions. To protect yourself from scams and fraudulent sellers, thoroughly verify the seller's credentials and cross-check their details with equestrian associations or online communities.

By considering all aspects of horse ownership, from initial costs to ongoing care, you can create a financial plan that supports your equestrian dreams while maintaining financial stability. This foresight not only enhances your buying experience but also sets the stage for a rewarding relationship with your new horse.

Step 7: Calculating your budget

This is the backbone of a successful horse purchase. It requires a detailed understanding of both immediate and long-term costs. Use this budget to plan and support your financial decisions carefully.

As horse ownership comes with ongoing costs beyond the initial purchase price, planning for both expected and unexpected expenses is essential.

One-Time Costs:

- Purchase price: $_____

- Vet check / pre-purchase exam:$_____

- Tack and equipment: $_____

- Transport: $_____

- Other_____

Ongoing Costs:

- Agistment/boarding: $_____per month

- Feed and supplements: $_____per month

- Farrier: $_____ every 6-8weeks

- Vet care (routine and emergency): $_____ per year

- Insurance (optional): $_____per year

- Lessons/training (as applicable): $_____ per month

- Other _____

- Total Estimated Monthly Cost: $_____

Step 8: Identifying reputable sellers and breeders

Finding the right horse goes beyond evaluating the animal itself; it begins with identifying reputable sellers and breeders.

Trustworthiness and credibility are the cornerstones of a successful purchase. So, how do you know if the seller is reliable?

Seller reputation checks become vital. Investigate their history and look for consistent patterns of honesty and integrity. References and testimonials from previous buyers can offer a glimpse into their experiences. Ring previous owners of a horse or other buyers. They provide invaluable insights into the seller's practices and the quality of the horses offered. A reputable seller will likely have a track record of satisfied clients willing to vouch for him.

His reputation assures you of the horse's quality and enhances your confidence in the purchase, reducing the anxiety often associated with such a significant decision.

Professional networks are indispensable in locating reputable sellers and breeders. Recommendations from trainers or fellow riders who know the industry well can lead you to trusted sources. These individuals often have their ears to the ground and can provide insider information on where to find a quality horse that matches your needs.

Networking at equestrian events is another fruitful avenue. Horse shows, clinics, Pony Club, and competitions are not just about the event; they're opportunities to engage with the community, gather information, and build relationships. Conversations struck up in these settings can yield contacts and insights that might otherwise remain elusive. Cultivated with care, this network can become a valuable resource, offering support and guidance long after the initial purchase.

Evaluating breeders follows a similar vein but requires a closer look at specific traits and practices that signify reliability and quality. A responsible breeder commits to maintaining high standards in horse care and breeding practices. Their facilities should reflect this commitment— clean, well-organized, and indicative of a nurturing environment for horses. The condition and calmness of the horses speak volumes about the breeder's dedication.

Healthy, well-cared-for animals suggest a breeder who prioritizes the well-being of their stock over all else. This care is evident in the horses' demeanor, health, and overall condition. So if possible, visit the facility to observe these factors first hand. This will give you a clear picture of the breeder's operations and ethos.

Building a long-term relationship with breeders can reap benefits for the future. A strong relationship with a breeder can open doors to exclusive opportunities, such as the first pick of a new foal or insider knowledge about potential sales. They will sometimes retire a broodmare that is reliable under saddle which they wish to re-home.

Regular communication keeps you informed about upcoming sales, new foals, and any developments in the breeder's program. It establishes a rapport that fosters mutual respect and trust, making future transactions smoother and more transparent. You can often put down expressions of interest in a particular mating or type of foal, even as an embryo!

Participation in breed events is another way to maintain these relationships. By attending open days, breed-approved auctions, or social gatherings hosted by breeders, you demonstrate ongoing interest and commitment. These interactions solidify your connection and provide opportunities to learn more about the breeder's philosophy and practices.

As you continue your search for the right horse, remember that the relationships you cultivate with sellers and breeders are as important as the horse itself. These connections form a foundation of trust and knowledge, guiding you towards making informed and confident decisions.

As you prepare to delve deeper into the buying process, these relationships can support you in evaluating potential horses, ensuring that your next steps are grounded in expertise and reliability.

There are many types of horses out there, with much overlap as to suitability. Knowing what you want, having patience, and perseverance are necessary to find it.

Just know that this means that the right horse for you will be out there.

***

I have extensive coverage of selecting horses in my book *"The Thinking Horse Breeder,"* where I talk about the handling and training of a young horse, its growing needs, and how we break in our young horses. Check out my website here for further information:

https://thinkinghorsebreeder.chalani.net/ or from bookstores worldwide

Chapter 4

Where to buy

Without breaking the bank or losing your sanity

B uying a horse is a bit like dating—you're looking for *the one* that fits your lifestyle, makes you happy, and doesn't break the bank. But just like dating, there are different ways to meet your horse match. Each buying method comes with its own set of joys and pitfalls, and this chapter is here to help you navigate them.

Private sale

A private sale happens directly between the seller and the buyer. It's the traditional way of buying a horse—often through word-of-mouth, online ads, or personal connections. It will usually involve a visit to the horse and conversations about the suitability and experience of the horse and rider. A responsible seller is checking you out, as well as you checking out his horse — if he doesn't do this, it might be a red flag that he doesn't care who the horse will go to, as long as he makes a sale. He might be negotiable on price if he wants a quick sale.

Pros:

- Personalized experience: You get to know the horse in its current environment and talk directly to the person who knows it best.

- Room to negotiate: Prices are usually more flexible, and you might be able to buy with a payment plan.

- Less pressure: You can take your time to assess the horse's suitability.

Cons:

- Subjective descriptions: Sellers might see their horse through rose-colored glasses (or conveniently forget to mention its quirks).

- Risk of being ghosted: Some sellers disappear when you start asking tough questions or sell the horse to someone else before you get a chance to see it.

- The person who regularly rides the horse may not be there for you to see it ridden.

Tip:

Sellers rarely give trials these days, so visit several times. See how the horse handles a few different situations, especially things it'll encounter in its intended job (trail rides, competitions, etc.).

Online platforms:

Specialized websites and social media platforms are now common marketplaces for horses. You'll find everything from backyard ponies to elite dressage stars listed online. Horses can be found for sale in magazine galleries and classifieds, Facebook, Craig's List, Gumtree, E-bay, and many other avenues of online advertising. Very few advertisements show professional photos, so picking out horses worth enquiring about can be hard.

Pros:

- Wide selection: You can browse horses from all over the country (or world) from the comfort of your couch or computer.

- Easy comparison: It's simple to filter by price, breed, discipline, etc.

- Convenience: You don't need to travel to view initial listings.

Cons:

- Catfishing: That stunning jumper might not actually be the same horse you see in person.

- Risk of scams: Scammers frequent these sites. Some sellers are less than reputable.

- No trial rides: Often, you're committing before you've even met the horse, to buy before someone else does.

Tip:

If you can't visit, ask for *recent, unedited videos* showing the horse in various scenarios (tacking up, loading onto a float, under saddle, etc.). Always contact the seller by *phone* to get a feel for the seller's tone, experience, and trustworthiness. And always do a pre-purchase vet check—*no exceptions*.

Private treaty

This method involves confidential negotiations, usually for high-value horses. Prices aren't advertised; buyers submit offers through an agent or directly to the owner.

Pros:

- Discreet: Ideal for buying or selling valuable horses without public scrutiny. Sometimes, bargains may be had because the seller doesn't want others to know they've sold a low-priced horse. You may be surprised, so ask anyway.

- Tailored transactions: The process is often more thorough, with time for vet checks, trials, and negotiations.

- Access to exclusive horses: You may find top-tier horses not publicly advertised.

Cons:

- Expensive: You're likely looking at horses in the upper price range, but not always, so give it a try if it meets your criteria.

- Time-consuming: Negotiations can drag on.

- Not for everyone: It's a niche market for serious buyers and sellers.

Tip:

If you're shopping in this market, chances are you're already experienced. But if you're not, hire an agent to represent your interests.

Expressions of interest

This simply means that a horse may be sold to the highest bidder, but there is nothing to say the seller *must* do this. You put in a bid and hope to be chosen, either because the seller believes you will be the best fit or because you have put in the highest bid.

EOIs may require a deposit to ensure you are a serious bidder, but returned if you don't succeed. (Always check first what the requirements are to lock in your bid). There will also be a deadline for bid submission, and a date you will be advised as to the successful bidder. You may even be given a "last chance at your highest offer" notification to reconsider whether you will offer a higher bid. This then becomes a silent auction.

Expressions of interest can be a useful way to buy, and you might be able to buy on a payment plan. Foals, embryos, and foals in utero are often sold in this way.

Which method is right for you?

Let's be real. There's no one-size-fits-all answer. It depends on what you're looking for, your budget,and your risk tolerance.

- First-time buyers: Stick to private sales with a trusted advisor by your side.

- Competitive riders: Auctions and private treaty deals might offer more options.

- Budget-conscious buyers: Online sales can yield great finds, as the price is usually listed, but tread carefully.

Buying a horse is an emotional roller-coaster. One day you'll feel like you've found your dream horse, and the next, you'll be convinced you've made a terrible mistake. But with a bit of knowledge and a healthy dose of skepticism, you'll end up with a partner that suits your needs—and hopefully your bank balance.

And remember, as with all things: *If it seems too good to be true, it probably is.*

Wanted advertisements

If you'd like to speed up the buying process, putting around a "Wanted" advertisement may be a good choice. Many horses become available if the owner sees an advertisement similar to something they have, yet hadn't gotten around to advertising it. This gives you the opportunity to pick up something without competition from other buyers.

If you are designing a wanted advert, make sure to include as much information as possible. Be reasonably specific so you don't get bombarded with unsuitable horses. Essential details would include height, age, breed or type, and the purpose. Give details as to the type of home which will be provided, your location, contact details and an idea of your budget. You don't need to include exact figures, but you must include a guide. Budget might be "healthy budget for the right horse" or "nothing over $8k." "Good home assured" is okay, but "Good home assured on family farm" would be better. You also need to state your must-haves, such as "must be good with traffic, dogs, and children." Unless you want to narrow your choices and pay a higher price, don't restrict yourself to a certain colour or sex of the horse.

Make sure you put a prominent heading, such as "Wanted to Buy" in bold. You can use a photo to attract attention if you like, but choose it carefully, with the caption "photo for attention only" if you do so.

Where should you advertise?

Putting out flyers on the noticeboards of local businesses, fodder stores, Pony

Clubs and the like, can be a useful method. However, you should probably place advertisements in dedicated equestrian or breed magazines which provide avenues for classified advertising and specialized sales. Although more costly, these will be more likely to place you before the right type of seller.

Another avenue is online sales platforms, which can be quite successful, but the downside is, viewers may miss seeing the advert amongst many others, and your advert might have a short life. Check out how long your advertisement will be visible compared with its cost. Here is an example: (ASH = Australian Stock Horse).

Wanted

Cool-minded all-rounder for keen teenager.
15.2-16h, reg ASH, 5-10 years
Must have basic dressage training, and jumping experience.
Pay to $12k. Located Victoria
Experienced home on 10 acres.
Contact: 123 456 789

Don't forget, you can always make an offer on a horse you see, even if it is not for sale; but have your checkbook ready, in case the owner agrees. Plenty of horses have changed hands after an offer was made that the owner could not refuse!

Other considerations before buying

Transportation permits and passports may be required to move horses across state boundaries or countries. These permits ensure that horses are transported safely and that quarantine and health certifications are up-to-date. Familiarizing yourself with these legal aspects and costs before purchase can prevent future headaches and ensure a smooth transition for your new horse.

You may not be able to travel a horse immediately after purchase, yet you still have responsibility for it. Make sure you book insurance which covers travel, as a first priority and add extra time for unexpected delays. I prefer to pay for a full year.

You will probably need to pay board for the days leading up to travel departure. However, the transport company will give you a single price for the entire trip to your property and require the money at the time of booking. Note: if you pay someone privately to travel your horse, check that they have a suitable float/trailer. If it is non-compliant with road laws, you could void your insurance.

Each area has its own set of laws regarding horse ownership and transport, and failing to comply can result in fines or legal issues. Zoning and land use laws dictate where to keep horses and what facilities to build. Ensure that you can legally house your new horse and modify your property accordingly.

When it comes to buying a horse, it's a journey.

A bit daunting, a bit thrilling—but absolutely life-changing when done right. My goal with *Buy the Right Horse* is to make sure every rider, breeder, and horse lover feels confident, prepared, and safe as they search for their dream horse.

But here's the thing: to get this book into the hands of more people who need it, I need *you*.

Why? Because your opinion matters! Most people decide to buy books based on reviews. A review is more than a couple of sentences—it's a bridge to help someone like you make a better decision.

What difference can you make?

Your review could mean:
* One more child finds a steady, safe horse.
* One more family brings home a horse they'll treasure forever.
* One more competitor finds a prospect who'll shine in the arena.
* One more breeder gets the perfect foundation mare for his dreams.

By sharing your thoughts, you're not just talking about a book; you're helping people avoid mistakes, feel empowered, and—most importantly—find their dream horse.

How can you help?

It's simple! Scan the QR code below or click the link to leave your review. It'll take less than a minute, but the impact could last a lifetime for someone just starting their journey:
https://www.amazon.com/review/review-your-purchases/?asin=BOOKAS IN

QR CODE HERE

If you've ever felt the joy of connecting with a horse—or the frustration of buying the wrong one—you know how important it is to get this right.

So let's do this together. Your review could be the one thing that changes someone's story — for the better.

Thank you, from the bottom of my heart.
Jeanette

Chapter 5

Buying at auction

Strategies for confident bidding

A uctions are high-energy events where horses are paraded around, and buyers bid against each other. You'll find everything from backyard ponies to top-level performance horses.

Auctions are great places to see what is available and to get an idea of breeds and current market prices.

There are two types of auctions:

High-end breed-specific or discipline-specific sales (such as polocrosse, showjumping, or campdraft), including National or State sales and Yearling Sales. These are where you can only buy horses of certain categories or disciplines. Horses are usually registered and perhaps eligible for promotional events or elite futurities.

These sales may only happen once or twice a year and may require long-distance travel to the venue to buy a horse.

Good performance horses and horses with potential can be found here. Horses are usually well-catalogued, inspected for suitability and presentation by the organizers, and demonstrated under saddle before the sale by the vendors.

Examine the printed conditions thoroughly so you know the buyer requirements and under what conditions (if any) you can cancel the sale.

Low-end markets or regional sales – anything goes.

From unhandled, nervous horses to green horses, difficult and unsound horses, malnourished horses and poorly bred horses, horses that will end up at slaughterhouses, to bargain buys and genuinely good horses (few and far between). Horses are often entered late, so may not be catalogued.

Pros:

- Fast transactions: You'll know by the end of the day whether you've secured a horse.

- Potential for bargains: Especially if you know what you're looking for and others don't.

- Exciting atmosphere: There's a thrill in bidding wars. You can learn a lot about the sales process, the lingo, and different types of horses by going a few times without bidding.

Cons:

- High pressure: It's easy to get swept up in the excitement and overbid. You may fail to get a horse and end up buying another less suitable one due to disappointment.

- Limited background info: You often won't know much about the horse's history. Sellers can have tricks and collusion to get higher prices.

- Buyer beware: What you see is what you get; very limited disclosure by sellers as to problems and suitability. You'd better have a good eye.

- No refunds: Once you've paid and taken the horse, it's yours, warts and all.

Tip:

Bring a knowledgeable friend to keep you grounded and help spot any red flags. Stick to your budget, no matter how much you feel for the skinny mare with her malnourished foal.

WARNING – Do not buy at auction, unless someone experienced is advising you on what to buy, such as your mentor.

I cannot stress enough that you should leave auctions for experienced buyers so you can take your time finding the right horse.

Before the auction: do your homework

- Set your budget (and stick to it). Write down your maximum bid—and I mean *MAX*. Auction fever is real, and your wallet will thank you later. You will soon forget the horse you didn't buy when you find the right horse somewhere else.

- Research the auction catalogue. Have you got your eye on a specific horse? Learn everything you can from the listing. Check breeding, performance history, and any available photos or videos.

- Ask for the vet records. If the auction house provides vet checks, review them carefully. No records? Be cautious and budget for your own post-sale exam.

- Bring a trusted horse person. Two pairs of eyes are better than one. Your mate can spot things you might miss (like a subtle lameness or a too-good-to-be-true sales pitch).

- Dress for the job. Wear comfy boots and weather-appropriate gear. Auctions aren't fashion shows, but you *will* be on your feet inspecting horses. You might want a comfortable cushion for seating.

Try before you buy - this is difficult at an auction.

At the auction: eyes open, wallet shut

- Arrive early to watch the horses. Pay attention to how horses behave in the yards and during handling. Are they nervous? Calm? Lame? You'll pick up a lot just from observing.

- Ask the right questions. Don't be shy. Ask the handlers about temperament, training, and quirks. But take everything with a grain of salt—they're there to sell. Read any information posted at the yard and in the catalogue (mark it with relevant information).

- Stick to the game plan. Do you have your shortlist? Great. Stick to it. Don't get tempted by shiny new prospects outside your budget or expertise.

- Pay attention to the auctioneer's language. Listen closely to how horses are described. Words like "prospect" or "needs experienced rider" often mean *project horse*. If you're not up for a challenge, walk away.

- Watch the bidding pace. Some auctions start slow and then speed up fast. Pay attention. The bidding rhythm works to avoid overpaying in a frenzy.

- During the bidding: keep calm and bid smart.

- Start slow. Let others set the pace. Jumping in too early can drive the price up unnecessarily. Have someone bid on your behalf, if you are nervous.

- Know when to walk away. If the bidding exceeds your budget, *walk away*. There will be another horse (and another auction).

- Don't get swept up in FOMO. Fear of missing out can be expensive. Stick to your pre-set limits, even if your heart starts pounding.

After the auction: buyer beware

- Inspect the horse thoroughly. Once you've won the bid, take a closer look at your new horse. Does it match what you saw earlier? If something looks off, get a vet's opinion *immediately*. Speak to the vendor about the horse, get his contact details, and any other pertinent information he's willing to provide. If the horse has paperwork, make sure you have it signed then and there so you can transfer it to your own name.

- Sort out transport. Check if you need a pass-out. Make sure you have a plan to safely get your new horse home. Auctions can be chaotic, and you don't want a stressed horse on your hands. Check your horse has plenty of feed and water while it is waiting to be collected.

- Insurance. Many auctions will insure at the fall of the hammer. Check that this has been done.

- Give your new horse time to settle. Expect your new purchase to be a bit frazzled. Let them decompress at home before jumping into training.

Red Flags

- The horse is "sold as-is" with no disclosures.

- The seller is not present or is "unavailable."

- The seller avoids eye contact or gives vague answers.

Assessing horse conformation - There are many training clinics for judging and assessments. Just ask your local club what is available. Xander Ide and Stewart Robinson. K8 Photography.

- The horse shows signs of discomfort, nervousness, or aggression.

- Bidding escalates unusually fast (could be shill bidding, where a seller uses a separate account or asks a colleague to bid, thus artificially raising the price. In most places, it is against policy and illegal.)

- Descriptions like "needs work" or "great potential" without proof.

Online auctions

These days, many auctions are combined with online bidding availability. This means catalogues are usually put out early with good detail so you can enquire with the seller about things like the suitability of the horse, its height, what it has done etc.

You can often get a feel for whether the horse will be out of reach so as to cross it off your list. The seller may be willing to give you his reserve.

You must register before you make your bid, and with most, you can record your lowest or highest bid, or simply wait until the horse enters the ring to make your bid like an in-person auction.

Online auctions usually allow you to watch by live stream so you can see exactly what is happening, without having to go in person.

Other sales are organized by breed associations without a combined live auction, simply with a closing date for bids, so the horse remains on the seller's property until sold. You are relying on photos or video to assess the horse. You might even find one in a location near you and save on travel.

"There's no such thing as a perfect horse, but there's definitely such a thing as a bad deal. Bid wisely!"

***

Chapter 6

Buying horses in partnership

Understanding group ownership models

O wning a horse is a dream for many, but the reality is often expensive, time-consuming, and demanding. Between purchase costs, training, daily care, and competition commitments, full ownership can be overwhelming, especially for those with limited time or financial resources.

This is where shared ownership comes in. By partnering with others to own, care for, and compete with a horse, you can enjoy the rewards of ownership without the full burden. Whether through a private arrangement with friends, a structured syndicate, or a corporate investment, shared ownership provides flexibility, affordability, and community.

Shared horse ownership: A smart solution for time-poor and budget-conscious owners

Horses require daily attention, from feeding and rugging, to training and exercise. For professionals, parents, or anyone with a packed schedule, this can be impossible to manage alone. Here's why shared ownership can be the perfect solution.

- Shared responsibility: With 2-3 owners, riding, training, and care schedules can be divided, ensuring the horse is well cared for without one person shouldering the entire workload.

- Flexible riding and competition schedules: Owners can rotate riding days or agree on who competes when, making it easier to balance horse time with other commitments.

- Less stress, more enjoyment: Instead of feeling guilty about not having enough time, owners can relax and enjoy the experience, knowing the horse is in good hands even when they're busy.

Example: A working professional and a university student co-own a horse. The student rides on weekdays, while the professional competes on weekends. Both get the benefit of riding without the pressure of full-time care.

Financial sharing: making horses affordable

The cost of horse ownership goes far beyond the purchase price. Ongoing expenses include agistment and stabling, feed and supplements, veterinary and farrier, tack, equipment and insurance, training and competition fees.

For many, these costs are too high to manage alone. Shared ownership divides the financial burden, making it possible to afford a higher-quality horse, better training, and superior care.

- Lower initial investment: Instead of buying outright, owners can split the purchase price, opening access to higher-caliber horses.

- Shared monthly costs: Boarding, feed, vet care, and training costs are divided, making elite horse ownership financially feasible.

- More resources for success: With pooled resources, owners can afford better trainers, transport to competitions, and top-quality gear.

Example: A group of three friends buys a promising young showjumper. By splitting the costs, they can afford top training and competitions, giving the horse the best chance of success, and split the workload.

Other key benefits of shared ownership

- Social and emotional support: Horse ownership can be isolating, but shared ownership builds a sense of community, with partners celebrating successes and supporting each other.

- Skill sharing: If one owner is experienced in training while another excels in horse care, each contributes their strengths, benefiting the horse.

- Exit flexibility: If circumstances change, it may be easier to sell a share than an entire horse, reducing financial risk.

- If a breeding stallion, he may receive better opportunities at stud from multiple owner's mares, and better promotional opportunities.

Final Thought: Whether you're short on time, watching your budget, or seeking a supportive community, shared ownership makes horse ownership possible, practical, and enjoyable.

Group horse ownership: Making expensive horses accessible

Buying a top-tier horse, whether for showjumping, eventing, dressage, or racing, is an exciting but financially daunting prospect. Elite horses can cost anywhere from tens of thousands to millions of dollars, making sole ownership out of reach for many buyers. But there is a solution.

Group ownership models, such as syndication and corporate ownership, allow multiple people or entities to invest in a horse together. This makes ownership more affordable while sharing costs, responsibilities, and risks.

But how does it all work? What are the benefits, risks, and key things you need to know before diving in? Let's break it down.

Why group ownership?

The benefits:

- Affordability: Instead of shouldering the full cost of purchasing and maintaining an expensive horse, group ownership lets you own a share at a fraction of the price.

- Reduced financial risk: Horses are unpredictable. Under-performance, injuries, or unexpected costs can be devastating for a solo owner. In group ownership, expenses and risks are spread across multiple investors.

- Access to higher quality horses: By pooling resources, a syndicate or corporation can afford to purchase top-tier horses that individuals might not be able to buy alone.

- Professional management: Many group ownership structures involve experienced trainers, syndicate managers, and bloodstock agents who handle the logistics, making ownership less stressful for members, particularly those with limited experience owning a horse.

- Shared experience: Ownership isn't just about the horse; it's also about the thrill of competition, or race-day excitement, stable visits, and special privileges, like entry to member only venues. Syndicates often build strong communities of like-minded enthusiasts.

- Potential returns: If the horse succeeds in competition, breeding, or resale, syndicate or corporate owners can earn prize money, sponsorship revenue, or profits from selling the horse.

The risks involved:

- No guarantees on returns: Horses are not a guaranteed investment. Even with the best bloodlines and training, not every horse will succeed in competition or have resale value.

- Ongoing costs: It's not just about buying the horse. You'll also need to cover training, vet bills, competition fees, and transport. These costs continue for years in sports like showjumping or dressage.

- Decision-making conflicts: What happens if some owners want to sell but others don't? Or if disagreements arise over training, competition schedules, or financial contributions? Governance and agreements must be clear.

- Long-term commitment: Unlike racehorses (which often retire young), equestrian sport horses can compete for 10+ years. If you join a syndicate, make sure you're in it for the long haul.

- Exit challenges: If you want out, how do you sell your share? Some syndicates allow transfers, while others may require a unanimous vote to sell the horse.

How group ownership works

There are two main models: Syndication and corporate ownership. While they share some similarities, they have different structures and purposes.

Syndication: Shared ownership among individuals

A horse syndicate is a group of individuals who buy shares in one or more horses. Each member owns a percentage of the horse and is entitled to their share of prize money, resale value, and other benefits.

Syndicates must be registered with the relevant governing body or society such as the FEI. A syndicate manager usually oversees the day-to-day operations, including trainer selection, vet care, transport, and finances. Some syndicates provide regular updates via videos, exclusive reports, or stable visits, while others operate at arm's length.

Members typically contribute to three types of costs:

- Initial Share Price – The cost of buying into the horse.

- Ongoing Expenses – Monthly costs covering training, care, and travel.

- Unexpected Costs – Vet bills, injury recovery, or prolonged training periods.

Some syndicates bundle everything into a single monthly payment, while others require you to pay bills from multiple sources. Any winnings or earnings are distributed based on percentage ownership. Some syndicates also take a management fee before distributing funds. If the horse is sold, members receive their proportional share of the profits. However, if you want out early, your ability to sell your share depends on the syndicate agreement.

Know what you're signing up for!

Corporate ownership: A business-driven investment

In corporate ownership, a horse is owned by a business entity rather than individuals. This structure is more common among professional stables, sponsorship-backed teams, or high-net-worth investors looking for strategic opportunities or tax benefits. (Think Budweiser Clydesdales.)

Unlike a syndicate, where decision-making is shared, a corporation owns the horse outright and makes all key decisions. Corporate ownership can involve prize money, sponsorships, corporate branding, breeding rights, resale, or tax strategies. If the horse isn't performing, the company may sell the horse quickly or use it for breeding, sponsorship branding, or client entertainment.

Key players in group ownership

Regardless of ownership type, certain professionals play key roles in managing the horse's career:

- Syndicate manager / Corporate executive – Handles decision-making, finances, and communication.

- Trainer – Responsible for the horse's training and competition schedule.

- Veterinarian and farrier – Ensure health, soundness, and shoeing.

- Bloodstock agent (if applicable) – Helps select the horse at auctions or private sales.

What to check before joining a syndicate or corporate ownership

- Who picks the horse? (Is the bloodstock agent reputable?)

- Who will train the horse? (Experience matters.)

- Where does your money go? (Should be a **Trust account,** not a personal one.)

- What happens if the horse is sold, injured, or retired?

- Can you exit the ownership easily?

What happens if there is a disagreement?

Disagreements are not uncommon in group ownership. Here's how they're typically handled:

- Syndication agreements – These legal contracts outline decision-making procedures, voting rights, and exit strategies. If there's a major conflict, the syndicate manager usually has the final say.

- Corporate ownership – Since the company owns the horse outright, corporate executives or directors make all key decisions, reducing the risk of disputes.

- Arbitration and mediation – Some agreements include dispute resolution clauses to handle conflicts professionally.

Is group ownership right for you?

Syndication is best if you want affordable, shared ownership with a social experience.

Corporate ownership is ideal for businesses looking for branding, investment, or strategic opportunities.

Before jumping in, do your research. Check the syndicate manager, trainer, financial terms, and contract details such as the PDS (Product Disclosure Statement) or Deed of Sale.

> *Owning a high-performance horse is a dream of many, but with the right approach, it can be an achievable reality.*

***

Buy any one of these three books here:
https://books.by/app/bookstores/jeanette-gower or from Amazon

Chapter 7

Assessments

The power of seeing what's truly there

N ow we go into much more detail about checking over a horse. Use each assessment to draw up your own checklist or just use the ones provided.

For first time buyers - this is where a lot of the mistakes are made. There must be emphasis on learning before buying and finding connections in the horse industry by having lessons, visiting and joining local pony clubs as non riders, finding out about dodgy dealers and the like. Do not go into this without doing your homework!

Behavioral assessments

Understanding horse behavior helps you make smarter, more confident choices.

When evaluating a horse, look for key behaviors that reveal its character. Horses are incredibly perceptive, picking up on things we often miss. How they handle new environments speaks volumes. A calm, curious horse adapts well; great for anyone who needs to transport frequently. On the flip side, excessive sweating, restlessness, or constant calling out can mean trouble with change.

Social skills matter too. A horse that stays relaxed around people and other horses is easier to manage and train; ideal for families or young riders.

Simple tests can tell you a lot. Take the lead rope test: does the horse follow smoothly, or does it resist? Groundwork exercises also show its training level. Watch for responsiveness to commands like halting and backing up.

Consistency is key. A reliable horse reacts predictably in different situations. Try small changes. Alter its feeding time or introduce a new handler. A horse that stays steady under shifting conditions is a solid choice for trail rides or camping trips.

And don't just assess a horse once. Visit several times if necessary, at different hours. Energy levels and behavior shift throughout the day, and a thorough look prevents surprises.

Checklist 1: Temperament and behaviour

Groundwork observations

- Observe how the horse reacts to approach and handling. Does it come willingly or shy away?

- Check the horse's manners during grooming: Does it stand quietly or fidget?

- Watch how it responds to being led: Does it walk calmly or pull and resist?

- Test the horse's reaction to objects (clippers, plastic bags, flags, poles?)

- Assess the horse's loading behaviour. Does it willingly enter a float?

- Observe how the horse interacts with other horses and people.

Under-saddle observations

- Check the horse's reaction to mounting: Does it stand still or move off?

- Evaluate its response to basic aids (walk, trot, canter, gallop, halt).

- Assess how it handles transitions: Are they smooth or resistant?

- Note if the horse spooks easily or remains calm in different environments.

- Note its performance with the tools of its work, e.g. a polocrosse pony should demonstrate its ability to handle stick and ball work with appropriate ease and athleticism; a stock horse with a stockwhip following cattle.

- Test the horse's willingness to work: Does it seem eager or lazy?

- Evaluate the horse's attitude after work: Does it return to a calm state or remain tense?

Red flags

- Aggressive or defensive behaviour (flattening its ears, biting, kicking)

- Excessive nervousness or spooky tendencies.

- Inconsistent behaviour between different handlers or riders.

Conformation and soundness assessment

Understanding equine conformation is key. It directly impacts a horse's movement, performance, and long-term soundness.

Ideally, the limbs should be straight and well-proportioned, with each joint aligning seamlessly to the next. Straight, well-aligned limbs reduce injury risk. Misalignment stresses joints and ligaments, leading to chronic issues.

Soundness, joint flexibility and freedom from lameness, determines a horse's suitability for work and longevity. Flexibility allows complex maneuvers and adaptation to terrain, while stiffness signals potential problems. For buyers, soundness is crucial—an unsound horse not only fails to meet its intended purpose but also poses a financial risk and heartache.

Body balance matters. A "downhill" horse (hindquarters higher than withers) may excel in speed sports like barrel racing but lacks comfort for hours in the saddle. An "uphill" build suits dressage, enhancing stride and collection. Polo ponies need short backs and daisy-cutter strides for speed and agility. Proportional features, like matching shoulder and hip lengths, contribute to stamina and athleticism.

A step-by-step approach is necessary to evaluate a horse's conformation effectively. Stand back and assess the horse's posture. Does it stand squarely on all four legs, or does it lean over its front legs, or worse, its back legs?

Check its head and neck proportions. A well-proportioned head and neck adds to the horse's aesthetic appeal and influences its balance and control. Check the horse's teeth. (Ask the owner to show you his horses' mouth.) You are looking for parrot mouth, missing teeth and the like, though you will still need to have a dental check later if you decide to buy.

The neck should be of good length, allowing for adequate movement and flexibility. Next, assess the back and top line. A strong back supports the weight of a rider and enhances the horse's endurance, while a level top line (neither uphill nor downhill) contributes to overall balance and posture. A sagging or uneven top line can indicate potential issues with strength or alignment, impacting the horse's performance and comfort.

Stand behind the horse to note if one side seems uneven compared with the other. Does the pelvis appear pointy? Are the hocks straight and strong? Cow hocks, where the hocks turn inward, can lead to increased stress on the hind limbs, affecting the horse's ability to push off and balance. This flaw can be particularly problematic for disciplines requiring powerful hindquarters, such as jumping or cattle work.

These assessments provide a comprehensive overview of the horse's physical capabilities and potential limitations.

Another concern is swayback, characterized by an excessive downward curve in the back. It often results from poor muscle tone or genetic predisposition and can affect the horse's ability to carry a rider comfortably, and may make fitting a saddle difficult.

While some flaws can be managed with proper training and care, others may limit a horse's suitability for specific tasks. Despite the ideal, many horses exhibit minor conformation flaws that don't affect their performance or health, *for the purpose you require.*

Few horses are flawless, but understanding conformation helps you weigh strengths and weaknesses. Bringing along an experienced horse person ensures a thorough assessment. Remember – No horse is perfect, but careful evaluation helps you decide what's manageable and what's a deal-breaker.

Checklist 2: Conformation and soundness

Overall conformation

- Check the head for symmetry, a kind eye, large nostrils, and mobile ears.

- Observe the neck and shoulders for correct proportions and a gentle arched curve into the throat.

- Evaluate the back: Is it straight and strong or dipped and weak? Will it fit a saddle well?

- Look at the legs: Are they straight and well-aligned, lumpy or smooth?

- Check the hooves: Are they well-shaped, with good heels, and healthy? And teeth: Nothing noticeable?

- Assess the hindquarters for strength and even muscle development.

Soundness check

- Watch the horse walk and trot on a flat surface: Are the gaits even and smooth?

- Look for swelling, heat or lumpiness in the legs.

- Check for signs of lameness: Does the horse favor one leg or show stiffness?

- Ask the seller about any previous injuries or surgeries.

- Have a veterinarian perform a pre-purchase exam, including dental. (This can be delayed until you are about to make a final decision.)

Red flags

- Uneven gaits or visible lameness.

- Tripping, stumbling, dragging feet.

- Hoof cracks, thrush, seedy toe, or poor hoof condition.

- Swelling, heat, bumps or major scarring on legs or joints.

- Conformation flaws that could cause long-term soundness issues.

- Postural signs: leaning forwards with back legs trailing, leaning back.

- Grumpiness, ears pinned, tail swishing – these may indicate pain or discomfort.

Training level and potential assessments

A horse's training level affects both its performance and how well it matches your skill set. A well-trained horse can provide confidence for a novice, while an experienced rider may prefer a greener horse to develop.

A horse lacking key skills will need time and investment to bring up to standard, which is critical if you're looking for a project or a schoolmaster. Knowing where a horse stands in its training journey helps you set realistic expectations about the effort required to fill in those gaps. Training gaps matter when you are purchasing a competition horse, as these may need to be worked through.

Gathering background information is essential. Performance records reveal not just achievements but also exposure to different environments and challenges. Watching the horse in training gives further insight. Does it respond willingly, or does it resist? Has it been trained with methods that align with your approach? Could you confidently take a horse back to basics if needed? For example, if a dressage horse has been trained with rollkur, do you have the skill and under-standings to retrain it?

Beyond current training, consider the horse's potential. A willing learner with a calm, curious approach to new tasks is more likely to progress. Past improvement in skill, even in a different discipline, suggests adaptability and continued growth.

Your experienced instructor can spot subtle strengths and weaknesses, tailoring recommendations to support both you and the horse. Their input helps lay the groundwork for a solid partnership, ensuring you start on the right path, whether for resale or long-term ownership.

Checklist 4: Training level and potential

- Ask for a demonstration ride by someone familiar with the horse.

- Evaluate the horse's response to basic commands: walk, trot, canter, gallop, and halt.

- Test the horse's obedience to lateral aids (leg-yield, shoulder-in, etc.).

- Observe its reaction to new challenges (poles, small jumps, trail obstacles, unfamiliar areas).

- Assess the horse's willingness to work – does it appear to enjoy its job? How often is it ridden?

- Check if the horse stands quietly for mounting and dismounting.

Evaluating potential

- Ask about the horse's previous training history. Who trained it, how long was it in training, and for what purpose?

- Discuss the horse's competition experience (if relevant).

- Check if the horse's age and breed suit your needs (e.g. younger horses for growth potential, older horses for reliability).

- Evaluate the horse's attitude towards learning. Is it curious and eager or resistant?

- Confirm the horse is physically suited to your discipline. Does it have the movement for dressage, the scope for jumping, lightness for polocrosse?

Red flags

- Inconsistent performance between riders.

- Resistance to basic commands.

- Fear or anxiety during training exercises.

- Overstated claims about the horse's abilities.

- The horse appears to be shut down, over-worked, over-drilled or robotic.

Registration and paperwork assessments

Registration with the umbrella organization will be mandatory for a competition horse, so make sure this has already been done and is current to avoid an impediment that may cost you time and money to proceed.

Check that the individual's papers match the description for brands and markings and microchip if it has one.

Also, view the registration certificate for any documentation of inherited genetic diseases. Some breeds will do mandatory tests at the time of registration, and the result will be marked on the registration. If it turns out the horse is positive for any of them, you may consider this a deal breaker; alternatively, it may be manageable under certain regimes. Discuss this with both the seller and your vet.

If the animal is to be used in the future for breeding, ensure that the horse is registered with its relevant breeding organization and that its breeding certificates are up to date in accordance with society requirements, such as sire registrations and service certificates.

If these are not up-to-date, you may find out that there is a reason for this, for example, the current owner is not a member in good standing or has let it lapse, signatures cannot be obtained, or paperwork has been lost.

All this complicates the transfer process later and is very expensive. Proper documentation ensures you're buying a horse with verified identity and history and saves you headaches later. Better to find out now and walk away, if it seems too complex.

Check list 5: Registration and paperwork

Registration papers

- Ask to sight the horse's breed registration papers (if applicable).

- Verify the horse's identity matches the papers (microchip, brand, or markings).

- Confirm the ownership details on the papers match the seller's information.

- Check if the horse is eligible for any breed or discipline-specific competitions.

Transfer of ownership documents

- Request a bill of sale or purchase contract that outlines the terms of the sale.

- Ensure the contract includes both parties' details, the horse's details, and any conditions of sale.

- Ask for any insurance policies currently in place and whether they can be transferred.

Health and vet records

- Ask for the horse's veterinary history, including vaccination and worming records.

- Request details of any previous treatments or surgeries.

- Confirm the horse's current diet and care routines.

Performance and breeding records

- For competition horses, request performance records to verify achievements. Check genetic tests for genetic diseases.

- For broodmares or stallions, in addition to performance records, ask for breeding history and offspring records. Check genetic tests for genetic diseases.

Red flags

- Missing or incomplete paperwork. If buying from a deceased estate, this may prove especially difficult. Who is to sign over documents?

- Discrepancies between the horse's description and its documentation.

- Reluctance of the seller to provide a bill of sale or contract.

- Unwillingness to disclose or discrepancies in veterinary history, or information on genetic tests.

With a clear picture of training history, adaptability, and professional insight, you're ready to make a decision that aligns with your ambitions. As we move forward, the focus will shift to the practical aspects of navigating the buying process, where we'll explore negotiation, legal considerations, and securing the best terms for your purchase.

Caution about drugged horses:

A horse that seems unnaturally quiet, sluggish, or "dull" may have been sedated to calm it down, or given painkillers to mask lameness. Get a blood test pre-purchase exam with drug screening, if you're serious about the purchase.

Signs include:
- Droopy lower lip, penis dangling, gait lacking coordination.

- Half-closed eyes or an almost trance-like state.

- Delayed reactions—slow to respond to touch, sound, or movement.

- Aloofness—not interacting normally with people or other horses.

Rookie mistake

"I drove 6 hours to see a horse (3 there and 3 back). Owner said he's got a small bump on his leg. I should have asked for video of it. But I was too eager to get there because all the ones I had liked to that moment were getting sold within days and I was able to get there to see it because I was on holidays. "I got there and the small bump turned out to be larger than a golf ball on the leg/fetlock with a large cut/scar and the horse was not even sound. I didn't even ask them to get it out of the paddock. "The moral to this is one person's small bump is a career-ending bump to someone else. So now I ask whether it has any blemishes and if so to send me pictures or photos before I jump in my car and drive for hours." – Lisa

Not safe but "been handled by kids"

"The owner didn't ride the horse due to a broken toe etc, been handled by kids, horse's bridle had the bit in back to front, horse bit handler when asked to lead. Owner kept lunging the horse because she was too scared to get on - he actually got worse the more she lunged him. Tried to rear when I put my foot in the stirrup. Oh and sorry there's nowhere to work the horse but he's safe to ride down the road! The list goes on.

"Lesson learned? The condition of the property, such as gear lying around, unsafe fencing and gates, is often a good indication of the horse's training (or lack of)." – Sandy

Could only travel in a truck

"I applied to an advert in Horse deals to a well bred filly (unbroken). I had video of horse sent to me moving freely in a dressage arena so I took the trip interstate with horse float and after an hour of being shown related progeny and the dam, I agreed to take her. I gave a full reference like the seller wanted and then I was refused due to having a horse float not a truck. So we came to an agreement that I would source a truck so I came all the way back home with an empty float.

Lesson learnt? It pays to ask more questions in advance of traveling to look at a horse. – Lorraine

No helmet

Went to view a medium trained dressage horse who had been out of work "for a while" but quiet and easy to bring back in to work. First red flag - the owner "didn't have her helmet" with her to work the horse first. She lunged horse under saddle. No humping, quite lazy in fact. So being young and dumb and thinking myself invincible I hopped on.

Well. That horse bucked like I have never seen a horse buck before. I got absolutely drilled. The worst part! The horse attacked the owner. I think he saw his chance and took it. I was lucky to not end up in hospital. The owner ended up in hospital to check for concussion, breaks and had badly injured hands (from defending herself). – Rebecca

Sarcoid

I bought a mare sight unseen. She arrived with a sarcoid the size of my hand on her hindquarter. I rang them immediately and they said they had never noticed. They refunded me but I lost the $1600 in transport as I paid for transport both ways.

Another one was a weanling stud colt that arrived with a large hernia. Same deal, got a refund but lost about the same in transport costs since I paid to return him as well.

Lesson learned? Get photos of each side prior to purchasing sight unseen. – Bec

***

Chapter 8

Forewarned is forearmed

Avoid surprises later by asking the right questions now

Y our excitement is mounting. You've just found a horse that checks every box—and deep down, you know this could be the one.

How do you go about making enquiries when answering the advertisement?

If you've followed all the steps in the previous chapters, you'll know in advance which things are the most important to you and which are deal breakers.

Enquire promptly, but take your time to process what you learn.

As you take this journey of speaking to sellers, you will begin to get an idea of what is available, the price range, what sellers are asking *you*, and the language they use. It becomes a learning curve so that you can formulate exactly what you want or *need*. (Slightly different.)

Ask lots of questions after reading the advert in FULL. There is nothing worse than a seller spending time answering questions that were in the advertisement already.

Use the list below to write down the seller's answers when you make your preliminary enquiries. Most sellers prefer you to enquire by phone, as this gives them an indication that you are serious. However, if an advertisement says enquiries by Facebook, Messenger, or email, use their preference out of courtesy and ask for a phone number to follow up for more detailed information.

Here is a standard enquiry line when you first ring. Write the answers alongside each question.

"Hello [your name, from town/state]. I am inquiring about the 10-year-old bay gelding 16 hands you advertised in [name of media]. Is this horse still available?"

Now, if you are going to question the price or something else already in the advert, ask first so that you don't waste the seller's time. *"Is this horse's price negotiable? Is this horse a true 16h (Is it officially measured)? What is the date of birth on its papers?"*

If the horse is registered, ask if the registration is current and all fees are paid. Don't be fooled by a *pending* registration. [This may incur additional costs to *you*. In reality, it may not even be pending!]

Then tell them a little about yourself so that you can let the seller know why you have chosen to enquire about this horse.

"I am looking for a quiet horse for my husband, who only rides on weekends and has been riding off and on for about five years. We keep our one horse on agistment, and a new horse would be kept there with it and visited daily."

This gives the seller some idea about whether the home might be suitable, and allows him to ask you a few questions. He may answer some of the next questions himself, before you need to ask, or he may quiz you for more details. It is NOT sufficient to say, you LOVE your horse and he is your fur-baby and you will give a forever home. This is a big turn-off for a seller.

If the horse is as good as the seller says, he will want to know your circumstances.

Some of the questions may seem like doubling up, but ask them anyway. Have a pen and paper handy, date the conversation, and write the seller's name, phone number, and name of the horse. If the seller gives you additional information write that down too. You want to discuss this with your mentor/instructor/partner, etc. If enquiring about several advertisements, you may not remember all that was said about each horse.

- Where did you get it from, and what has it done before you bought it?

- What have *you* done with it?

- Why are you selling it?

- What is it like to ride? What level of experience is the current rider?

- What level of rider is suitable for this horse?

- How often is it ridden? When was it last ridden?

- Do you have to lunge it before being ridden or after a spell? (BIG NO unless you are experienced)

- What is its level of training?

- Where have you taken it? What has it been exposed to?

- How is it in traffic?

- What is its present condition?

- Has it been measured?

- Are photos available, and when were they taken?

- Is there any video (or can they take some ridden in the next few days) demonstrating movement and some of these points?

- Is there anyone else going to look at the horse? (*You'd like to know if you're first in line or down the list*).

Now's the time to seek more nitty-gritty after the initial questions. You want to know the horse is uncomplicated or at least that you are able to deal with any quirks or idiosyncrasies.

- What is it like to catch? Rug?

- How is it to tie up? (*Stands quietly, pulls back, reliable*)

- What is it like to float? (*Check how it loads. Is it okay with a horse next to it in a two or 3-horse float?*)

- What are its ground manners like? (*Strong, fidgety, pushy, gentle, etc.*)

- What are its feet like? (*Very good, must be shod, etc.*)

- How is it for the farrier, and how often? (*normal is 6-8 weeks*)

- What is its current paddocking situation? (*mares/geldings, group/alone etc*)

- Does it stand quietly to be saddled and mounted?

No horse is perfect, so what you are looking for is honesty or evasiveness of the seller and if there are any things that you can overlook or are non-negotiables for you.

Red Flags:

- Temperament – *Head shy, shies, kicks, bucks, pig-roots, girthy?* [These could indicate behavioural or medical problems]

- Alone – *Is it okay to ride alone without causing a problem away from its mates? How is he if his mate is taken out of the paddock?*

- In a group – *Calm, flighty, goes through water, kicks other horses, easy-going?*

- What are its legs like? *Injuries, sprains, scars, straight, sound?*

- Has it ever had colic, ulcers, or other serious illness? [*If yes, treatments, etc, explore with their vet if it could recur.*]

- Ask if the horse has been tested for genetic diseases and what the results were. *

- Is it a good eater or a good doer?

- When was dental and worming last done?

- If a mare – question if "marish" or "alpha" – if so, ask them to describe the behaviour they are talking about as people have different ideas as to what it means. (*top dog, nasty/bossy with others, especially over food.*)

- Does it have any vices like windsucking or fence-walking? *

- What is it like around children, dogs, or machinery? (*Move this question to the top of the list if you're looking for a child's pony or family horse.*)

- Ask if anyone else knows the horse who can give a reference about the horse (e.g., local club/instructor/breeder). Ring them to ask what they know about the horse. Ask some of the same questions as above.

- Search Google / Facebook with the name of the horse and seller and see what information is out there, such as a previous ownership and photos.

If you are somewhat of a beginner and don't know what some of these terms mean, make sure you do your research and learn. Take someone you trust with you.

CAUTION: If you are buying an unadvertised horse, for example if you are buying a horse which you have known and ridden for a while, say from a Riding School, still go through the checklist. The horse may have had multiple riders, and been ridden every day of the week. What if you can only ride it once a week? It is important to tick as many things as possible on your list.

REMEMBER: the purchase cost of a horse is only the start of ongoing expenses. If you buy something because you feel sorry for it, you may be up for thousands of dollars in care before you have a happy, healthy horse. It still may not prove suitable.

Chapter 9

Viewing the horse

Evaluation, vetting, and final considerations

B y now, you should know if you are interested enough to arrange a ride. Let the seller know you will talk to your mentor or instructor, to organize a time to visit.

IMPORTANT: Get back to the seller within 24 hours with an answer and time. Don't leave him hanging!

Be polite – Put yourself in the seller's shoes! *It may be an especially sad sale.*

For safety's sake: you will want to see the horse ridden first by its regular rider before you hop on. Check before you visit that this rider is available to ride the horse. Additionally, the less experienced you are, the more important it will be to take your instructor or mentor with you to ride the horse as well.

Take your helmet and boots.

You need to ask the seller to demonstrate what the horse can do in its home environment. If you want a performance horse, you should also ask for its record and/or watch it perform at a competition. **View the horse from each angle: front, both sides, behind**. Watch the horse being caught, trotted up and down, saddled, bridled, lunged, and/or ridden, then put back out with its friends.

Watch its obedience, manners, personality, conformation and movement, general handling, and group behaviour.

Caution: If when you arrive, the horse is already saddled and waiting for you, this could be a red flag. The horse could be difficult to catch or have been ridden earlier to make it quieter for you when you ride it.

After watching it being ridden through its paces, decide if the horse's education is at the right level for you and if you feel comfortable having a ride. Ask any more questions you have as you go along. Expect to spend a couple of hours.

Do you feel emotionally drawn to the horse? Does it show interest in you? Does it have a "kind eye?"

You must feel like the horse is one you can establish a rapport with, not just that it ticks your boxes.

If it is branded or registered, check that its age matches what you were told, or have its teeth checked.

Then thank the owner for his time, and give him a time by which you will get back to him, for example, the next day. Don't leave the owner hanging!

The test ride

A test ride offers a unique window into a horse's temperament, a critical factor in determining if it's the right fit for you. As the seller saddles up, focus on how the horse handles it. Does it wriggle or stand still? Does it remain relaxed when asked to perform tasks or when encountering unexpected obstacles? This ability to stay calm under pressure is particularly necessary for beginner buyers and those seeking reliable schoolmasters. A horse that responds to commands with precision and willingness suggests a good temperament.

Observe how it reacts to cues. Does it quickly understand and execute instructions, or does it hesitate, showing reluctance or confusion? This may be more a reflection of the rider's level than that of the horse. A responsive horse is easier to train and safer, especially for leisure riders and parents looking for a pony for their child.

To maximize the information gathered during a test ride, consider varying the settings in which you ride. Try different environments—an arena, a trail, or an open field, to see how the horse adjusts. Riding in varied settings can reveal a lot about a horse's adaptability and comfort level.

Test various gaits—walk, trot, canter— to provide further insight into the horse's smoothness and responsiveness. Pay attention to transitions between gaits; a horse that moves fluidly from one to another is often more balanced and easier to control.

For buyers focused on performance, make certain the horse is shown to you in the discipline you are buying it for. For example, a reining horse should be able to demonstrate all the movements required of a pattern with ease and fluidity; a showjumping horse should show some boldness and rounding of its back over various types of jumps. A campdraft horse should have seen cattle in camp, mustering or at feed lots, and be considered "cowy," whilst a polocrosse horse should be handy with a stick and ball and comfortable amongst other horses.

During the ride, look for indicators of suitable manners. A horse that remains calm under saddle, even when faced with distractions, shows a desirable level of maturity and training. Willingness to work is another positive trait. This suggests that the horse has been well-treated and trained.

A horse eager to please and engage with its rider signals a positive attitude, making it a pleasant companion for leisure and competitive activities. This can be shown by its interest in its surroundings and its curiosity about new people and objects.

A horse that shows little interest may be overworked, sedated or in pain.

Recognizing red flags

It's imperative to stay vigilant for warning signs that may indicate potential issues. Resistance to commands, ears back, tail swishing, or head shaking/twisting are red flags. If a horse repeatedly ignores cues or requires excessive coercion, it might be a sign of underlying behavioral or training problems. Anxiety or nervousness is another concern. A horse that appears jittery or skittish could be reacting to unfamiliar surroundings or past trauma, which might require additional time and effort to address.

Be mindful of these signs to ensure that the horse you choose meets with your expectations and capabilities.

A horse that displays hostility, such as biting or kicking, suggests possible deep-seated behavioral problems, fear or discomfort. Such aggression might stem from improper training techniques, where the horse has learned to associate humans with negative experiences, or from health issues such as ulcers or kissing spine.

It's essential to understand that horses, as prey animals, rely on flight for survival and may become defensive if they feel threatened.

Another concerning behavior is unpredictable spooking. While all horses may react to sudden stimuli, a horse that frequently snorts at objects or spooks for no apparent reason could be struggling with eyesight issues, or anxiety or fear, potentially due to past trauma or mistreatment, or simply lack of exposure in its training.

This behavior might not only disrupt training but also pose safety risks, especially for leisure riders or families with young children. Such horses need to develop confidence in their rider, so are not suitable for nervous riders.

The roots of problematic behaviors can often be traced back to their environment or history. Improper training techniques that lack consistency or employ harsh methods can lead to a distrustful and reactive horse.

Past trauma, whether from mistreatment or a significant accident, can leave lasting scars on a horse's psyche. These experiences shape how a horse perceives people and new situations, often categorizing them as fearful. Poor behaviour loading onto a horse float is typical of a fearful horse.

Environmental factors, such as inadequate socialization or lack of mental stimulation, can exacerbate these issues, leading to vices like cribbing or weaving.

Recognizing these causes helps understand the horse's behavior and assess its potential for rehabilitation and training.

Ask specific questions about the horse's history, handling experience, and any known behavioral challenges.

If you encounter red flags, it's important to have a plan for addressing them. Consult with your mentor to assess whether they are deal breakers or whether they might easily be resolved with further instruction. Transparency from sellers is vital in making an informed decision. Honest communication about any behavioral issues allows you to assess the situation realistically.

Be upfront about your concerns and expectations. Seller disclosure agreements can formalize this transparency, ensuring that all known issues are documented and acknowledged. A trustworthy seller will be forthcoming with information, recognizing that a well-informed buyer is more likely to provide a suitable home for the horse. This openness not only builds trust but also sets the stage for a smoother transition and integration of the horse into its new environment.

Exercise:

- Note the horse's response to new environments. Does it remain calm or show signs of stress?

- Observe interactions with people and other horses. Is the horse friendly and cooperative?

- Conduct a lead rope test and note the horse's willingness to follow commands.

- Perform groundwork exercises with obstacles, if possible, to assess focus and compliance.

- Visit the horse several times at different locations, noting any changes in demeanor.

After the ride:

When you ride, have someone take a video so you can discuss it with them or send it to your mentor. If all goes well, you will discuss it on the way home and promptly get back to the seller with an answer.

If unsure, let them know what you're unsure about and discuss further.

If the answer is a definite no, let the seller know then and there, saying that you have decided the horse isn't the right fit for you. Don't say something like "The horse is too tall" when you knew it was 16 hands from the first advert!

Maybe arrange another visit.

If you are trying to decide between two horses, *be upfront.* Tell the seller that you are going to look at another horse and will let them know then. Suggest when by, so they are not left hanging. If you don't have an end time, you will likely lose to another buyer, and the seller will see you as a time waster.

Some sellers will allow a 7-14-day holding deposit, but you must be clear whether this is refundable. You can also request to buy the horse subject to a veterinary check within this time frame. Note: most sellers will not agree to a trial but may agree to further rides on the property within this time period. This can be very helpful for you to try out your own gear on the horse and have a few lessons before collection.

Sometimes, despite your best efforts, the terms simply don't align with your needs or budget. Advise the seller. In these instances, having the courage to step back is essential. Walking away doesn't necessarily mean the end of negotiations; it often signals to the seller that you're serious and informed, potentially leading them to reconsider their position.

The veterinary check or pre-purchase examination

If you decide to take the horse, will the seller be happy with a vet check? (You don't have to do one, but if the seller says "no", that is a red flag.)

If it is a riding horse:

A vet check is highly recommended! In this process, the seller must usually sign a declaration that the horse is free of drugging or medical intervention at the time of the examination, which offers you some protection.

If possible, be present at the examination. Discuss with the vet what you are looking for and what the seller has told you. A vet check should establish *suitability for your level and needs.*

The vet will establish identification, look at the legs for serviceability and soundness, check teeth for age and health, and assess eyes, heart, lungs, movement, and conformation overall. He should ask to see the horse lunged and ridden if you are buying a competition horse.

Additionally, requesting a veterinary examination can rule out health-related causes for a behavior, such as pain or neurological issues. A thorough check-up might uncover physical discomfort that explains a horse's irritability or unpredictability, providing a pathway to address and resolve the behavior.

Your own vet usually does the pre-purchase exam, but you can sometimes get the names of several vets in the seller's area and choose one. It is not recommended to use the seller's own vet due to conflict of interest. The examination is done before the conclusion of your trial of the horse, paid for by you, the buyer.

A standard pre-purchase exam encompasses several critical components. It begins with a physical examination, where the vet assesses the horse's general condition, checking vital signs and body condition and examining the horse for any visible abnormalities. This physical exam also includes an evaluation of the horse's gait, looking for signs of lameness or stiffness that might indicate underlying issues.

The examination will hopefully find anything you may not have seen which requires further investigation. If you are looking for a performance horse, you are well advised to have blood tests and a comprehensive x-ray examination as well. The higher the horse's value, the more this will be essential, and indeed, it may be necessary for insurance as it establishes a baseline before any possible claims.

Diagnostic imaging, such as x-rays, radiography, or ultrasounds, can gain deeper insights into the horse's musculoskeletal health. These images can reveal conditions like joint problems, bone abnormalities, or even early signs of arthritis that might not manifest visibly yet.

Blood tests provide insights into the horse's internal health. They can detect infections, metabolic issues, or other systemic problems that could affect the horse's long-term well-being and performance. If you're traveling interstate to purchase a horse or paying a lot of money, I'd try to have bloods taken on the same day you saw it or minimum next day afterwards. I know of too many instances when the horse was sedated for the test ride and then turned out to be unsound. Even if the vet merely sits the bloods in a fridge in case of disputes a week or two later.

This thorough approach ensures that no stone is left unturned, offering a comprehensive understanding of the horse's health.

Selecting the right veterinarian to conduct the pre-purchase exam is as important as the exam itself. Experience with pre-purchase exams is important, as these exams require specific skills and knowledge to interpret subtle cues accurately. Look for a vet who has a proven track record with these exams, ensuring they know what to look for and how to evaluate the findings.

Familiarity with the breed or discipline is another consideration. For example, if you are looking at a potential endurance horse, a vet who has experience with endurance rides is a logical choice.

Different breeds have unique health profiles and risks; a vet who understands these nuances can offer more tailored insights. A vet well-versed in the specific discipline you're interested in can better assess the horse's suitability for that activity, considering both health and performance factors. This specialized knowledge can be the difference between a good purchase and an exceptional one.

If it is a breeding horse:

Get a breeding soundness examination and a clear swab, or if thought to be in foal, a pregnancy test, especially before traveling the horse.

Interpreting the results of a pre-purchase exam involves a careful evaluation of risk versus reward. Not all findings are deal-breakers; some may be manageable with proper care and treatment. It's about understanding which issues are minor and which might pose significant risks.

The vet will provide clarity. He can explain the implications of each finding, helping you weigh the potential long-term impact on the horse's health and usability. A candid discussion with your vet will provide a clearer picture of what to expect in terms of care, management, and possible future complications.

This collaborative approach ensures you make an informed decision, balancing the horse's health prospects with your needs and expectations.

Veterinary evaluations are an added cost, but so is buying the wrong horse for the purpose you require it for.

The sale

Immediately after discussing the matter with the vet advise the seller if you are going to proceed or not.

It is your responsibility to have all your financials sorted *first*, especially if you must get a loan to pay for the horse. Do this before viewing the horse, (and any other matters, such as discussing with your husband.) Do not expect the seller to accommodate you. Your financial readiness may be the difference between you securing the horse or not.

If you can't afford the horse OR must seek your husband's permission to get a new horse, do not make enquiries in the first place!

Don't expect a seller to hold a horse for you. Don't disappear off the radar and give yourself a bad name for being a "time-waster." Word spreads.

Then discuss what arrangements you will make for the horse's collection. This needs to be within a suitable time frame, or the seller will likely charge agistment.

Once paid for, the horse is your responsibility, not the seller's. If an injury occurs, you will be charged fees for medical treatment, extra care, and the like. The higher the price of the horse, the more you should consider insurance from the moment of sale.

To sum up

- Do your research – don't believe everything the seller says. [*They may not know, or they were told inaccurate information.*]

- Don't exaggerate your abilities or experience.

- Arrive on time. If a cancellation is necessary, re-book with an apology. *Don't be a "no-show" for the seller.*

- Don't expect the seller to keep a horse for you, so ask what the conditions of sale are and whether you are first in line.

- If you're buying sight unseen (*not recommended*), try to get videos, referrals, and information from past owners.

- Don't drag the process out unnecessarily. Don't leave the seller hanging!

- Remember, you don't own the horse until you have paid for it (with a cooling-off period).

- You can't return a horse just because you have changed your mind. (Consumer Protection Act)

- Make sure you understand if a deposit is refundable or not. If you pay in cash make sure you get a receipt.

- Ask for a contract of sale, especially if you are paying on a payment plan.

- If the horse is a giveaway, buy it for $1 and obtain a receipt as the new legal owner. [Otherwise, you run the risk of the owner demanding it back later, saying it was a lease.]

- It is not hard for you as a buyer to say, "I'll think about it and let you know in 24 hours if I want to go any further." Again, don't leave the seller hanging. Thank them for their time.

- In a hot market, you may need to make a snap decision. This is why your prior research, financial readiness and market knowledge means *everything.*

CONGRATULATIONS ON YOUR PURCHASE
Go home and celebrate with relief and expectation of a dream come true!

Chapter 10

Selecting the breeding horse

Hard truths before you commit

When considering horse breeding, it's important to recognize that each breed offers distinct traits that can shape the success of your program. These genetic traits are the foundation upon which breeding decisions rest and must fit your specific discipline, whether for sport, show, or leisure.

Each breed has unique strengths, which, when understood and harnessed correctly, can produce offspring that excel in their intended field.

The compatibility of breeds with specific breeding objectives is critical. If your goal is to produce a top-level sport horse, you might focus on breeds like the Irish Draft, Dutch Warmblood or Hanoverian, known for their exceptional performance in dressage and showjumping. These breeds have been selectively bred for traits like power, precision, movement and calmness.

Show qualities of conformation, movement, and presence, are also significant. Breeds like the Arabian, Thoroughbred, Morgan and Riding Pony, with their striking appearance and presence, captivate judges and audiences alike in the show ring.

The Australian Stock Horse emphasizes balance, sturdiness, utility, and versatility, appealing to a wide range of disciplines, such as polo, campdrafting, the hack ring and challenges. Thoroughbreds make amazing hacks, eventers and polo ponies. Quarter horses are the Western specialists and their placid nature makes them especially good for hunting, camping and trail riding.

Breed *Standards of Excellence* are written up for all the major breeds on their websites. It is a breeder's duty to understand and select horses in alignment with the Breed Standard. These are the traits that set the breed apart from all others. Therefore, you must choose a breed with standards that meet your own.

Understanding breed-specific traits allows you to choose a breed with the genetic potential to fulfill your breeding vision, ensuring the best possible outcomes.

All breed standards emphasize structural soundness and balance, as they influence the horse's performance and long-term health. Breed standards are there for a reason, and should not be changed or diluted to make way for something flashy or fashionable.

Breeding responsibly and professionally requires experience with both the chosen breed and the discipline *before acquiring breeding stock.*

It is also a very long-term journey to breed horses, filled with hopes, dreams, and huge challenges along the way, which cannot be underestimated.

> *Please do not breed unless you seek quality and excellence in your breeding programme.*

A horse with strong breeding potential should yield the benefits of passing its desirable traits and characteristics to its offspring. Each foal confirms the original horse's value, and if chosen well, the foals should command good prices.

Evaluating breeding quality involves more than just observing the horse in front of you. Start by learning the correct jargon. Note that a horse is *by* (sired by) a certain stallion, and *out of* (born out of) a certain mare. If you get it the wrong way around you won't be considered a serious breeder.

Pedigree analysis is vital, as a horse's pedigree provides insights into its genetic potential. Horses from lines with proven success in each generation, are more likely to pass these qualities to their offspring. Your selections should be based on a balance of genetic traits, (especially genetic disorders), breed-specific strengths and weaknesses, and the compatibility of these elements with what you strive to produce.

Performance records further inform this decision, providing a history of achievements and capabilities. A mare or stallion with a solid track record in competitions or shows brings credibility to your breeding program. Check out the offspring of proven stock to see how they measure up in competition and with breed standards.

Local considerations also influence breeding decisions. Climate adaptability is an important factor. Certain breeds thrive in specific environments, and understanding these preferences can ensure the well-being and productivity of the horses. For instance, the hardy Shetland and Welsh Pony is well-suited to colder climates, while the Arabian, with its origins in the deserts of the Middle East, and Ahkal Teke of Turkmenistan, may fare better in warmer regions.

The local environment influences not only the health and comfort of the horses but also the availability of resources such as grazing land and water. By considering regional conditions, you enhance the potential for successful and sustainable horse management.

A stud buyer should ask for a breeding examination of the stallion or broodmare and the results of any genetic tests that have been done as appropriate for the breed. In addition, if buying a mature stallion, tests should assess semen quality, and any other tests recommended at the time by your vet.

I do not recommend buying a horse that is unregistered and/or has not had its breed mandatory testing done. Especially check if sire registration and licensing of stallions is required by your Association, and if that has been completed. Full breed registration and owner membership in good standing are your peace of mind for valuable breeding stock.

Embarking on your journey to buy breeding stock can be thrilling yet overwhelming. The choices you make will define not just the quality of your herd but also your reputation as a breeder. Here's a step-by-step guide to help you make informed and ethical decisions, ensuring your foundation stock sets you up for long-term success.

Know your goals

The first question to answer is, *Why am I breeding?* Without clear intentions, it's easy to lose focus. Your goals will influence every decision, from the bloodlines you choose to how you plan your stud's growth.

- Purpose: Are you aiming to produce a specific type of horse — a show jumper, dressage champion, or a versatile all-rounder? The pedigree and conformation of your purchase should reflect this.

- Are you breeding for yourself or for sale, or a mix of both?

- Legacy: Are you laying the groundwork for producing one exceptional foal or a long-term breeding program?

- Be honest with yourself. Breeding requires commitment and vision, and "just because," or "the mare can't be ridden" isn't a reason to start.

- Understanding your breed's standard is crucial. This ensures your selections align with long-established benchmarks rather than fleeting trends. Build your knowledge first. Assess whether each prospect lives up to its breed standard.

Network and research

- Talk to mentors: Seek advice from experienced breeders about bloodlines, reputable sellers, and current market trends.

- Visit studs: Observe breeding operations and evaluate their stock.

- Read and learn: Breed magazines, pedigree databases, and conversations with seasoned breeders are invaluable resources.

- Speak to industry veterans: they often hold wisdom about older bloodlines and qualities that modern trends might overlook.

Cost-effective options

While price isn't always an indicator of quality, extremely low prices are often red flags. A quality performed horse may come with a higher initial cost, but its value will be reflected in your breeding program's success.

On the other hand, I have often been asked if I would take a mare, when the owner has finished with her. This is because the owner doesn't have the desire or facilities to breed with her. Sometimes an owner will do a deal with you, so you can breed the first foal, and the owner has the mare returned in-foal to your stallion.

Such deals are often cost-effective ways to obtain proven stock of different bloodlines, but you must ensure you have a lease contract for this purpose. What happens if the mare does not get in foal? Is there a live foal guarantee? What happens if the mare dies foaling? Do you need to sign a lease transfer with the breed association, in order to register the foal in your name?

Considerations:

- Leasing a mare or stallion: Leasing allows access to premium genetics without the up-front purchase cost. Ensure contracts are clear and the horse is registered with your breed association. What happens if a mare is returned for service after losing her foal?

- Older mares: Proven broodmares can be excellent investments, even well past their prime, and may better fit your budget. Those in-foal or with a strong breeding history are particularly valuable. Avoid mares that haven't foaled for a few years. Make sure you get a breeding soundness examination before proceeding if she is not already in foal.

- Full siblings and close relations to well-known performers may often make suitable breeding stock. However, they may cost almost as much to purchase as their well-known relation.

- Avoid horses that are unbroken or untried (unless due to a known injury) and without an outstanding pedigree. You simply don't know enough about the horse without it being performed. Until then, it only has "potential."

For the love of breeding (our cover foal with the Author.)

If you are taking a surrogate mare, because you are buying an embryo, the embryo must have parentage which fulfills the above considerations. The surrogate must be in good condition *and be easy to handle*. Her behaviour will influence the temperament of her foal!

When it comes to foundation stock, prioritize quality over quantity. Each animal you bring into your breeding program should meet rigorous standards.

Evaluating breeding stock

Pedigree and genetics

Pedigree is a roadmap to potential. A horse's lineage can reveal strengths, weaknesses, and predictability in traits like temperament, conformation, and performance. The horse must have strong bloodlines close up and in depth.

- What to look for: Proven sires and dams, consistent family success, and alignment with your breeding goals.

- What to avoid: Horses with untraceable or unproven / poor backgrounds, genetic disorders, or health and soundness red flags.

Conformation and temperament

Conformation refers to the horse's physical structure. It directly impacts performance, soundness, and longevity. Temperament is the horse's intrinsic nature rather than what it is like after successful training. Some horse's natures make them unsuitable for novices. Familiarize yourself with your breed's standard and choose horses that exemplify those traits.

Mares: the cornerstone of your program

The mare has a profound influence on her offspring and is the backbone of any breeding operation.

- Performance pedigree: Look for mares from strong maternal lines, where success is consistent across generations.

- Pedigree depth: A single standout in a pedigree isn't enough. Consistency across ancestors indicates reliability in passing desirable traits.

- Temperament and conformation: Temperament can make or break your program. A poor temperament, even in an otherwise perfect mare, can undermine your breeding program. Even a physically outstanding horse can be unsuitable if it has a poor attitude. Always consider the temperament you want in your foals. Is she easy to catch? If not, do you have the right facilities?

- Check out the mare's own performance record. This gives you an indicator of her abilities, trainability, and soundness. A well-performed mare in the field you are breeding for is valuable in your program. If a mare is untried, find out why.

- Ensure all mares intended for purchase are vet-checked for breeding soundness and screened for genetic disorders common in your breed.

- If in foal, does she come with a live foal guarantee, and is this transferable into your ownership?

The stallion: take your time

Rushing into stallion ownership is a common mistake for beginners. Instead:

- Use proven outside stallions for your first few breeding years. This allows you to focus on developing your expertise.

- Look for the best pedigree possible close up and with proven depth. Especially look for a horse with outstanding maternal lines. This differentiates him from others of the same sire lines.

- If you decide to buy, opt for an older, proven stallion with offspring you can evaluate. Look for consistency in passing on his desirable traits. Proven here means he is proven in the discipline as well as progeny proven in your chosen discipline, noting their conformation and temperament.

- Has he been collected? Who owns the semen and will sign certificates? Are there pending live foal guarantees to be honored?

Stallions require significant investment, skills, upkeep, and promotion. Only take this step when you're confident in your ability to manage the responsibilities.

Planning for growth

Start small

- Managing a large band of mares can quickly become overwhelming. For instance, a group of five mares means managing probably 5 foals, yearlings, and 2-year-olds alongside other horses. Scale your operation according to your capacity.

- Diversify your bloodlines. Diversity is critical when starting out. By investing in mares from varied backgrounds, you can identify the most successful crosses over time. Choose mares that are very similar in type, though they may be different in pedigree.

Common pitfalls to avoid

- Chasing trends: Breeding fads come and go, but breed standards are timeless. Stick to the fundamentals rather than being swayed by fleeting popularity.

- Overestimating your capacity: It's easy to underestimate the workload of a breeding operation. Factor in the time and resources required to manage your stock effectively.

- Ignoring performance in a pedigree: A pedigree filled with consistent, sound, and high-performing ancestors is a safer bet than relying on a single "superstar" in the lineage. If there is only one star, the horse is the same as the majority who have that single ancestor. The horse has nothing else attractive in its pedigree, and doesn't stand out for any reason.

Final checklist

- Find a mentor: Guidance from experienced breeders is invaluable.

- Do your homework: Study pedigrees, bloodlines, and breed standards thoroughly.

- Start modestly: Focus on a small, high-quality herd. Better to start out with two high-quality $20,000 mares than 5x $8,000 mares.

- Invest wisely: Prioritize mares over stallions; their influence on your program is longer lasting, and their quality separates you from other breeders.

- Plan ahead: Understand your workload limits and your property's capacity.

Breeding is a marathon, not a sprint. Success comes from patience, preparation, and a commitment to continuous learning. By focusing on quality, ethical practices, and long-term goals, you'll set the foundation for a breeding program that thrives for generations.

***

I have covered all aspects of choosing breeding stock in much greater detail in my book *"The Thinking Horse Breeder,"* available from Amazon.

or   https://books.by/jeanette-gower

If you live in Australia, you can buy a signed copy direct from me by going to: https://thinkinghorsebreeder.chalani.net/

Chapter 11

Legal essentials

Safeguard your rights and interests

Buying horses sight unseen: risks and rewards

M ost people will have bought or sold horses without requiring any form of sales contract or sales documentation. Sadly, those days where a handshake agreement was all that was needed, are becoming infrequent, due to the much higher value placed on modern horses, and the risk of dodgy sellers or scams.

In certain scenarios, purchasing a horse sight unseen may be the only viable option. Maybe you're dealing with a horse located in a distant region (or country) where travel is impractical or costly. Or perhaps you're considering a high-value competition horse famed for its performance, where the reputation precedes any physical inspection.

In these cases, relying on the seller's description and any available media becomes the norm. However, this approach comes with inherent risks. The primary concern is misrepresentation. Here, a contract of sale is invaluable. You may include a clause whereby the horse can be returned within 7 days (or 14) if it proves unsuitable (with vet certificate provided) or proves to be misrepresented. You can't return a horse simply because you've changed your mind.

Without a physical inspection, you might find discrepancies between what's advertised and reality, whether in the horse's condition or its capabilities. There's also the challenge of assessing temperament. A horse might appear calm in videos but could behave differently in person, especially in new environments or under stress. This lack of first-hand interaction leaves a gap in understanding the horse's true nature, which could lead to disappointments or challenges post-purchase.

To mitigate these risks, several strategies can be employed. First, insist on comprehensive video footage. Request videos that cover various aspects: the horse's movement in different gaits, interactions with handlers, and responses to common stimuli. These videos should be recent and unedited, providing a transparent view of the horse's behavior and abilities.

Engaging trusted local agents can also be invaluable. These agents act as your eyes and ears, conducting a physical inspection on your behalf, and arranging a veterinary check. They provide an impartial assessment, helping verify the horse's condition and suitability for your needs. This third-party perspective can bridge the gap left by your absence, ensuring that the information you receive is both accurate and complete.

Buying sight unseen has its advantages. Rare breeds often require searching beyond local markets, and purchasing remotely grants access to horses otherwise unavailable.

Time-sensitive opportunities are another factor. A horse with a strong pedigree or competition record may be listed at an attractive price for a limited time. Acting quickly without travel delay, can secure a valuable horse before others.

Once the horse arrives, post-purchase evaluations are essential. Start with an immediate vet check to confirm health and uncover any undisclosed issues. This protects your investment and prepares you for any necessary care.

Next, observe the horse's behavior. Spend time in different settings, assessing temperament firsthand. If a return is needed, costs are your responsibility.

Avoiding scams

These days the risk of being scammed is not just something that might "happen to someone else." Even in the horse industry one must be careful.

The main risks are fake websites (usually made by scammer groups in another country) and fake sellers who promote themselves on Facebook or other social media platforms.

I can do no better than to quote from Rachel Kosmal McCart from Equine Legal Solutions website: https://equinelegalsolutions.com/shocking-horse-sale-scam/

Buying horses on the internet

"If you're considering buying a horse sight unseen over the internet, here are signs you might be dealing with an imposter scam:

- The same horse is advertised on multiple websites at different prices.

- The seller will only communicate via email or text and won't talk to you on the phone.

- The seller won't provide additional photos or video when requested.

- The seller creates a sense of urgency.

- The seller is advertising a lot of horses for sale at once.

- The seller's horses are considerably less expensive than you would expect for horses of that breed and training level.

- The seller won't tell you exactly where their horses are located – (information necessary for you to arrange shipping after purchase).

- The seller appears to be in the business of selling horses but won't provide you with references from satisfied customers.

- The seller's website has links that go to blank or incomplete pages.

- The seller's website has content that seems odd (such as biographical information for someone other than the seller).

- The seller directs you to make payment to someone other than the seller.

- The seller directs you to make payment to a bank located in a country other than where the seller is located.

- The seller directs you to make payment via a method that seems odd, such as Western Union, or gift cards."

Trust Your Instincts. Overall, buyers should trust their instincts. If something seems fishy or too good to be true, it probably is!
Horse buyers and sellers can also educate and protect themselves by reading Equine Legal Solutions Buying and Selling Horses articles.

Understanding legal obligations and contracts

When purchasing a horse, the contract is your shield against future misunderstandings and disagreements. It's important to ensure that this document covers all necessary aspects to protect both you and the seller. If the seller doesn't provide you with a sales contract, you might consider drawing one up with your own lawyer. This is especially recommended the higher the value of the horse, and allows for returns should the horse turn out to be misrepresented or not "fit for use."

Begin by clearly identifying the horse. This includes the horse's name, breed, age, color, and any unique markings. Such details leave no room for ambiguity, ensuring that both parties are on the same page about the specific animal being sold.

Payment terms and conditions should be outlined meticulously. Specify the agreed price, payment method, and any installment plans, if applicable. This clarity helps prevent disputes over how and when payments are to be made, securing a smoother transaction process.

Seeking legal advice is a wise step to ensure the contract is robust and enforceable. A contract law specialist can offer invaluable insights into the nuances of transactions and help tailor the contract to your specific needs and local regulations. These professionals are familiar with the intricacies of horse trade laws and can identify potential legal pitfalls that might otherwise go unnoticed.

Reviewing local regulations is equally important, as each region may have specific requirements regarding horse sales and ownership transfers. Ensuring compliance with these regulations protects you legally and prevents any future complications that could arise from overlooked legal obligations.

Legal pitfalls in horse transactions can sometimes catch even the most experienced buyers off guard. Misrepresentation of a horse's history is common, where sellers may provide incomplete or misleading information about the horse's past. This can include undisclosed health problems or behavioral issues that surface after the purchase.

Breach of warranty is another potential pitfall. Sellers may unintentionally or intentionally fail to uphold guarantees regarding the horse's health or performance, leading to disputes and dissatisfaction. Being aware of these pitfalls allows you to address them proactively in the contract, including clauses that protect you from such eventualities.

If it is a broodmare in foal with a live foal guarantee, make sure this is covered in the contract. Does the seller own the stallion? If not, can the live foal guarantee be transferred to the new owner? Have embryos been collected and how many are held? If it is a colt sold for breeding purposes, make sure you have it covered if he proves infertile or crypt-orchid. If it is a stallion, are there any past contracts still to be honoured, such as live foal guarantees? Has semen been collected, and who has the rights? Make sure this is all recorded and you are clear as to your rights.

If a contract dispute arises, having a plan for resolution is crucial. Mediation and arbitration are effective alternatives to litigation, offering a less confrontational and often quicker means of resolving disagreements. These processes involve a neutral third party who helps both sides reach a mutually agreeable solution.

Legal recourse options remain available if mediation fails. It's important to outline these options in the contract, detailing the steps that will be taken should a dispute escalate. This foresight can save time and resources, providing a roadmap for addressing conflicts in a structured and fair manner.

Consider the case of a buyer who discovered undisclosed lameness in a horse shortly after purchase. The contract lacked specific health warranties, leaving the buyer with limited recourse. By engaging in mediation, the buyer and seller reached an agreement for partial reimbursement, avoiding costly legal battles. This highlights the importance of a comprehensive contract with alternative dispute resolution methods.

Purchase plan agreements

If you're buying on a plan, this document is not just a formality; it's your safeguard against future misunderstandings and disputes.

A well-drafted agreement meticulously details every aspect of the transaction. From the agreed price to the nitty-gritty of health guarantees, each element must be clear. Imagine the peace of mind knowing that every detail, from payment schedules to the transfer of ownership, is outlined.

Payment schedules should be realistic, allowing for manageable installments. Health guarantees offer reassurance, ensuring that the horse is free from major issues at the time of sale. Transferring ownership must be seamless, with all documents prepared to affirm your new status as the owner.

Stated in the contract should be when the documents will be transferred into your own name; usually within 30 days of final payment.

The complexity of these agreements can be daunting, and this is where legal counsel becomes invaluable. An equine lawyer can navigate the intricacies of contract language, ensuring that the terms are comprehensive and enforceable. They are adept at identifying loopholes that might otherwise be overlooked, protecting your interests.

The seller will usually provide the plan and a contract. Have your legal advisor check this over and advise you of its terms. He may recommend other clauses to insert before you sign. His expertise makes sure that your contract reflects not only your expectations but also the realities of such a transaction.

Once the terms are agreed upon, the document should be signed to gain legal validity. All parties involved, from the seller to the buyer, should provide their signatures. These signatures are more than mere endorsements; they signify mutual consent and understanding of the transaction terms. Witness or notary signatures further authenticate the agreement, adding an extra layer of security.

Even with a solid agreement, last-minute negotiations are not uncommon. As the final step approaches, new considerations might arise. Perhaps you wish to negotiate delivery terms, ensuring the horse arrives at a convenient time or location. Alternatively, adding contingencies for unforeseen issues, such as a subsequent vet check or trial period, can provide additional security. These negotiations require tact and clarity. Effective communication ensures that any last-minute changes are incorporated smoothly without disrupting the overall agreement.

Drafting your purchase agreement

To prepare for your purchase, consider drafting a simple purchase agreement. Start by listing key elements you want to be included, such as health guarantees and payment schedules. Reflect on any contingencies you might require, like a trial period or additional vet checks.

This exercise provides a template for discussion with the seller and legal counsel.

The purchase agreement is a formal milestone to protect your interests, ensuring that all parties understand and agree upon each aspect of the sale. This formality is a necessity for elite horses, a necessity for a horse of high purchase price, and invaluable for one bought sight unseen.

Here is a typical agreement to purchase on a payment plan:

AGREEMENT TO PURCHASE WEANLING BY PAYMENT PLAN

Name of Horse: Foaled   /   /   Breed Reg #:

Purchaser's Name: Ph No:

Postal Address:

Email: Breed Memb #:

Seller's Name: Breed Memb #:

Address:

Email: Ph No:

CONDITIONS

1.   Total price is $ First payment of $ will confirm purchase, and repayments thereafter are to be by direct deposit. Until the first payment is made, the horse may be sold to another party. Final payment will be no later than   / /   .

2.   The seller agrees to provide all handling up to weaning at approx. 6 months of age, including basic float loading training, worming/tetanus vaccination x2, hoof care, branding and registration with the [Breed name association], with general agistment included in the purchase price until weaning.

3.   The horse is purchased with all faults, if any. Any veterinary or unexpected costs relating to injury or illness are to be borne by the Purchaser.

4.   The purchaser shall take full responsibility for the care of the above-named horse including costs of feeding, medical and veterinary expenses, education and handling, worming, hoof care, and any other related costs from the date of weaning, including agistment at $ per day, until transport is arranged, and collection occurs.

5.   Until the final payment has been made, the above-named horse shall remain on the property of the Seller and ownership will not be transferred to the [Breed name association].

6.   Every reasonable care shall be taken by the Seller while the above-named horse remains on the Seller's property, but no responsibility is taken for injury,

sickness or death suffered by the above-named horse whilst so agisted and is entirely at the buyer's own risk.

7.   This agreement remains valid in the event of any injury or sickness suffered and survives the death of the above horse. In the event of death, all remaining amounts become due and payable. Insurance is therefore mandatory, and Purchaser to confirm to Seller with a cover note showing company contact details by / / .

8.   In the event of default, after one month, all monies paid by the Purchaser shall be forfeit to the Seller and the horse will become the property of the Seller and the horse may be re-advertised and sold. The purchaser will be refunded their payments only IF the horse is sold at the same price, (less any costs).

9.   Transfer of the Registration of the above horse with the [Breed name association] shall be made to the Purchaser within 30 days of receipt of the final payment. The new owner agrees to becoming a member of the [Breed name association] to complete the transfer.

10. The new owner agrees to showing/competing the horse only in its registered name.

11. This contract expressly excludes any prior representations and understandings.

12. **Payments:**

Commencement Date: .... This is the date on which the deposit is paid. Please keep your own records of payment.

> Full Price $
>
> Less Initial Payment $
>
> BALANCE DUE $

Balance payable in [x] installments of $ on or before   /   /   (collection date.)

Please deposit into bank account: BSB   Account #

in the name of   in equal monthly payments or greater.

Final payment is due on or before collection date. <u>Please Note:</u> Failure to pay by the due date may incur interest or default fee of $ whichever is the greater, for every seven days overdue.

Agistment: $ per week if not collected by due collection date by arrangement only.

Agreed Collection Date: /   /

This is the date on which collection/ possession occurs. Date of weaning will to be advised by seller but may depend on weather and other events out of our control. Collection to be   weeks after that when all handling is completed.

If any payment is not made by the final payment due date, this agreement shall lapse through default, and the horse shall become the property of the Seller.

A Tax Invoice will be provided upon final payment if requested.   Yes / No

GST is / is not applicable.

Any other conditions of sale are to be written here, or overleaf and initialed by both parties.

Purchaser's Signature: Date: / /

Seller's Signature: Date: / /

For lower-priced horses, don't expect a sales agreement, but do get a signed receipt with the words "purchased for.......(your stated purpose, e.g. breeding)". You can always bring a carbon copy receipt book to the seller, make it out in advance and have him sign it. Have him add his postal address, phone number and email to the receipt, for your future records. Add yours, and give him a copy.

> *If you buy the wrong horse without such an agreement, you will just have to make do, sell it on, keep it as a pasture ornament, or if it is dangerous or has severe medical issues, euthanase it!*

***

Equine Legal Solutions (USA) offer horse Purchase Agreements and Sale Contracts for sale and instant download, as well as a number of other equine contracts for purchase. https://equinelegalsolutions.com/

You can buy purchase contracts from HorseForce (AUS) cheaper than you can have someone draft one for you. https://www.horseforce.com.au/product-category/horse-force-contracts/

Chapter 12

After the sale

Ensure a smooth transition for your horse

O nce you've finalized the purchase, the next step is moving your horse home, a process requiring planning and foresight. Your priority is choosing a reputable transport company.

Look for one with longstanding transport experience, as they understand horses' unique travel needs. Reputation matters; check reviews and ask fellow horse owners. A reliable company will have well-maintained vehicles, air-conditioning and in-transit video for longer distances.

Trained staff ensure safety and comfort, helping to promptly recognize and address signs of distress or discomfort. Their expertise and staging facilities for long distance travel, provides security for the horse and reassurance for you as the owner. They will keep in touch with you throughout your horse's journey.

Preparing the horse for travel is equally important. You don't want the horse to develop travel sickness or pick up an infection. Depending on its age and experience, the seller should have familiarized the horse with loading and unloading, and practiced with short trips if possible, to create positive associations, particularly for young or nervous horses.

A pre-transport health check is essential. If the sale was completed quickly, this can coincide with the pre-purchase exam. A veterinarian should confirm fitness for travel and check for stress or illness signs like abnormal behavior, reluctance to eat, fever, or lameness. Any health concerns can then be addressed before travel.

A useful step is to ask the seller for a quick photo before loading, which records the horse's condition and absence of new injuries. A healthy horse is more likely to travel well, reducing complications.

Permits and documentation

Transporting horses across regions or countries requires paperwork. ID, Passports and Transport Permits may be necessary, depending on local regulations. Health certificates confirm the horse is free from contagious disease, fit for travel, and appropriately vaccinated. Some locations may also require sprays. Having all paperwork in order allows a smooth transition and peace of mind preventing delays or fines.

Make certain you understand what is needed throughout the whole process. If you are using a professional service or agency, this should be seamlessly organized by them, though some documents may need to be signed by you as the owner.

If transporting yourself

If you're transporting the horse yourself, preparation is even more crucial. First, check that your horse float or trailer is sound, insured, and registered—don't laugh, it happens! If the seller is transporting the horse for you, as sometimes happens, ask about his float.

On the other hand, if this is the first time you have purchased a horse, I don't recommend this be the first time you, or a family member, transports a horse, particularly in a brand new float!

A safe transport environment includes proper ventilation. Open the hatches to prevent overheating and ensure a comfortable ride. Horses are more likely to overheat, in enclosed spaces, so canvas rugs should never be necessary. We also float in travel boots as a precaution unless they are foals with their mothers. Secure partitions are equally important, providing stability and reducing shifts or falls.

Choose routes that minimize congestion, reduce transit time, and lower stress. Traffic is unpredictable, so plan alternatives during peak hour. You don't want to be caught being unable to unload in congested traffic, should an emergency occur. Traveling during cooler parts of the day or at night, especially in warm climates, prevents heat stress. Many horses travel better at night because this is their natural rhythm to rest.

For longer trips, plan quiet rest stops where the horse can relax and drink and even pick at grass. Many horses won't urinate in a trailer or drink well, increasing dehydration risk. Regular breaks allow stretching, urination, and recovery. Personally, I avoid traveling more than four hours without a break for the horse. Observe your horse during these breaks. Is it alert or lethargic? Such observations help adjust the journey to meet its needs.

If transporting a young horse, I recommend bringing a reliable horse or pony as a travel companion for the return trip. This calms the youngster and encourages eating and drinking.

Post-Transport Care

Once the journey ends, allow the horse time to rest and adjust. A quiet space minimizes travel-induced stress and helps it settle into its new environment.

Never put a new horse straight in with unfamiliar horses immediately after travel, especially late in the day when it doesn't know the fences or where to get a drink. This is an accident waiting to happen.

Quarantine *is* important. Keep the horse from nose-to-nose contact with others for up to two weeks to watch for signs of contagious illness, like strangles. Monitor behavior, appetite, and physical condition for any signs of lingering issues. Early intervention prevents minor stressors from becoming serious problems.

Incorporating these practices ensures safety, comfort, and a smooth transition.

Post-purchase paperwork

Once the excitement of acquiring your new horse settles, the task of managing the post-purchase paperwork begins.

Organize every document related to your purchase into files. These papers serve as a record of the transaction and provide essential information for future reference. Purchase receipts are the first items to organize. They confirm the transaction details and the agreed price as evidence of ownership.

HorseRecords

Health and vet records accompany these receipts, offering insights into the horse's medical history. Does it need worming or vaccinating upon arrival? Vaccination schedules, previous illnesses, or treatments are important for future veterinarian visits. Keep these documents in order so you can easily facilitating smooth communication with them or potential buyers down the line.

I recommend you use an online records system like HorseRecords, to transfer and file all your written documentation.

You can find out more about Horse Records here:

https://www.horserecords.info/

Why not give it a try? The first two horses are free.

Transferring legal ownership

This process involves notifying the relevant equine registry, which officially records the change of ownership. This transfer is essential for maintaining accurate records within breed registries, which may influence breeding potential and value.

Many times the seller just passes over everything to you in the expectation you will transfer the horse if you wish to do so. Sometimes it is better for this to occur than promises from a tardy seller. Get onto it immediately. Paperwork is easily lost, so often to the detriment of the horse, for it affects future traceability. Even if you think you will give your horse a 'forever' home, sh_ _ happens!

Microchip or brand registration may also be required. Micro-chipping provides a permanent identification method, linking your horse to you unequivocally. It's a straight-forward process, often a requirement in many regions for identification and theft prevention.

Brands, though less common nowadays, serve a similar purpose and were a traditional method of marking ownership. Ensuring these registrations are up-to-date protects your investment and records your member name as the horse's registered owner. Note: A certificate of registration is not *proof* of ownership. Only a bill of sale, or signed receipt into your name, is proof that a sale occurred into your name.

Most breeds now use online recording and transfer systems, so check online, to see if all has been finalized. If you are not sure what you need to do, contact your breed association for clarity.

Ongoing documentation is a task that doesn't end with the initial purchase. Regular updates to veterinary records are necessary, documenting any treatments, vaccinations, or health changes. In Australia, you will also require a PIC (property identification number) for wherever your horses are kept. Check your own region's requirements.

Training and performance logs are equally important, especially for showing the horse or on-selling. Documentation of milestones and progress tracks the horse's development and adds value by showcasing its capabilities to potential buyers or trainers. These logs serve as a testament to the horse's skills and achievements, providing a tangible record of its journey under your care.

Managing a file of documents can be daunting, but utilizing digital tools can simplify the process. Cloud storage solutions, like HorseRecords, offer a secure and accessible way to store important documents, so that everything from purchase receipts to health records is in one place.

These services provide peace of mind with automatic backups, protecting your records from loss or damage. Transitioning to digital management not only de-clutters physical space but also enhances efficiency, allowing quick access on your phone to any document when needed. Try it. The first two horses are free.

https://www.horserecords.info

Insurance and liability

Owning a horse is incredibly rewarding, but it also comes with its fair share of risks and responsibilities. That's where equine insurance comes in. It provides a safety net for the unexpected. Mortality insurance, for example, covers the horse's value in case of death, offering financial relief during an already difficult time and funds for buying another horse.

This type of coverage is especially important for high-value horses, ensuring your investment is protected. On the other hand, medical and surgical insurance helps cover for illnesses or injuries. Horses can face sudden health issues, and these policies ease the financial burden of treatment so you can focus on their recovery rather than worrying about the cost.

The benefits of insuring a horse can go beyond just health coverage. Insurance also protects against theft or loss. If your horse is stolen or goes missing, you won't be left without options. Accidents are unpredictable, but whether it's a minor injury in the paddock or something more serious requiring surgery, insurance gives you peace of mind knowing you're covered.

Start by comparing different policies to make sure they align with your horse's value and intended use. Some policies even offer extra benefits, like coverage for alternative therapies or rehab support. Read the fine print so you understand exactly what's covered and what's not. Some companies will not ensure beyond age 15. Keep in mind that different horses have different needs. A schoolmaster will likely require different coverage than a broodmare, for example. Doing thorough research and consulting with an insurance advisor will help you find the best protection for both horse and equipment.

It's also worth checking whether you can add equine coverage to your existing property insurance. It might be more cost-effective than purchasing a separate policy. Look into whether a higher excess could lower your premium. You may be able to get this under a business name and have tax benefits.

Liability insurance is a must-have for horse owners. If your horse interacts with the public, whether through boarding, lessons, or trail rides, you have legal responsibilities. Liability coverage protects you from claims if your horse injures someone or damages property, such as if it gets loose and hits a car. This is especially important for those who host events or allow others to ride their horses. If an accident happens, this insurance can help protect you from costly legal consequences.

For additional protection, consider having waivers for guest riders. These should be clear and detailed, outlining the risks involved in riding or handling your horse. Having properly drafted waivers in place can help prevent legal issues down the road. It's a good idea to consult a legal advisor to ensure your waiver is comprehensive. If members of the public visit your property, putting up a clear sign at the entrance can also help reinforce these precautions.

Take the time to secure the right insurance coverage. Then you can focus on what really matters, enjoying your horse without unnecessary financial stress. By understanding your options and planning ahead, you can ensure both you and your horse are well protected in any situation.

Settling your horse in

Bringing a new horse home is exciting, but a little preparation makes all the difference.

Start by setting up a clean, safe space, whether that's a stable or yard, ensuring secure fencing, plenty of room to move, and soft bedding for comfort. Have fresh water ready and stock up on hay, hard feed, and any necessary supplements. Find out ahead of time, what the previous owner's routine and feeding regime was. If you need to make adjustments, do it gradually over a few days.

Give your horse time to settle in. Let it explore its stable and paddock first, watching how it reacts. Once it seems more comfortable, slowly introduce it to other areas. Horses take comfort in familiar landmarks like fences and water troughs, so letting them find their bearings at their own pace helps them relax. Walking them around the property can also build confidence without pressure.

Meeting new horses should be just as gradual. A slow, structured approach keeps stress levels low and helps your horse feel safe.

Keep an eye on eating, drinking, and behavior. A horse that's pacing, sweating, or calling out excessively may need extra reassurance. Stick to a calm routine. Offering quiet company, and even a few treats can go a long way in helping it settle.

Patience is key; some horses take longer to settle in. Many will walk fences or not associate well with others for weeks.

Routine care

Bringing a new horse home is a thrilling moment filled with promise and potential. Yet, it also marks the beginning of a crucial phase where you and your horse must adapt to one another and the new setting. Imagine stepping into a new workplace with unfamiliar faces and routines; it's overwhelming, isn't it? Horses being creatures of habit and instinct, experience similar reactions when introduced to new environments.

Horses thrive on consistency, finding comfort in knowing what to expect. Establishing a routine is fundamental to helping your horse adjust.

Daily feed and exercise schedule provides structure. Consistency in your handling, such as grooming or training sessions reinforces a sense of normalcy. This structure not only aids in the horse's adjustment but also strengthens the bond between you. Over time, these routines evolve into a seamless part of daily life, creating an environment where the horse feels safe and confident.

Next, establish routine veterinary care as a cornerstone to your horse's well-being and longevity. Regular health checks play a vital role in preventing diseases and maintaining optimal health. Annual dental work and vaccinations are key to these checks, offering protection from common illnesses such as influenza and tetanus, dental disease and ticks. Vaccinations should be administered in consultation with your veterinarian, who can tailor a schedule to your horse's specific needs and regional risks.

Alongside vaccinations, parasite control programs are important. Parasites can severely impact your horse's health, leading to weight loss, colic, and anemia. Regular fecal tests can help determine the type and quantity of parasites present, guiding the appropriate de-worming strategy. Unfortunately, it is not simply a matter of buying a tube of wormer and giving it to them. Many worm types have become resistant to the chemicals in wormers, so you need a careful and proactive approach as guided by your vet.

You can download my free worming scheduler here: https://jeanettegower.gumroad.com/l/kdarbm?

Arrange farrier visits as soon as possible, but most importantly, within the first six weeks of purchase. The saying "no hoof, no horse" underscores the significance of hoof health. Horses require regular hoof trimming and, in some cases, shoeing to maintain balance and prevent issues such as cracks, splits, or overgrowth.

Trimming schedules depend on the horse and its environment but typically occur every six to eight weeks. A skilled farrier can identify potential hoof problems early, such as thrush or laminitis, and address them before they escalate. Proper hoof care not only contributes to your horse's soundness but also enhances its performance and comfort, making farrier services an indispensable part of your care routine.

Keep in touch with your mentor and the local community. Participate as much as you can. Involve yourself in continuous learning.

Don't hesitate to reach out for help when needed. Speak to the past owner or your mentor. It can make all the difference. Professional guidance can provide the additional support to navigate through behavioral issues, paving the way for a successful transition and a fulfilling relationship between you and your horse.

Scouring foal

Bought a foal. It arrived in terrible condition and with scours. Lucky I quarantined it. 2 weeks later it was still scouring. My daughter suggested if it was a goat, she would say Coccidiosis. So I took a fecal sample to the vet. Results: This foal had a similar bacterial infection. The vet said it was lucky to be alive. It was in quarantine for months. – Janelle

Yarded horse

What sounded like my perfect horse was advertised. I took the money and float 5 hours to buy this horse, after asking the owner to not catch the horse before I got there. When I arrived the horse was in a round yard. At that stage I expressed my displeasure.

Then on examination the horse was experiencing a "tying up" episode. (Could not walk.) So I left. The man was so angry, I was nearly running out the gate in fear. Going to his local saddlery on the way home I told the staff about the horse. They told me it was this person's practice to starve and restrict water as a way to break a horse's spirit; that he often did 50k rides on these horses before people came to look at them.

No wonder the horse had tied up. He had obviously ridden that horse a long way to be in that condition when I arrived. – Kylie

Dream stallion

About 12 or so years ago I paid $6000 for a stallion for my stud. He was my dream horse and it was sight unseen. I took out a loan for this horse as 6k was a huge amount for me back then. The deal was the woman selling him to me would drive him to a friend's and then a truck would pick him up from there. The day she was due to drive him there I got a text to say she couldn't do it. She couldn't part with him, even though I had paid in full. I was devastated.

She offered me a mare in foal to him for 2.5k so I took her and the rest of my money back. The mare foaled a nice colt but not what I wanted for a stallion so I arranged to have him gelded. He died during the procedure.

To make matters more frustrating, 2 or 3 months after she "couldn't part with him" she offered him to me again for the same price. I couldn't afford him them and I wasn't about to go through that again. Lesson: Make certain the seller is mentally ready. – Kylie

Chapter 13

Real world experiences

What can we learn?

The unhandled brumby

The first horse I purchased was an unhandled brumby. I was a teenager at the time, and though I had handled and broken in some horses, I had never handled a brumby. It was the summer school holidays, so I was looking for a project to resell. I answered a classified advertisement for an $80 2-year-old (not knowing at the time it was a brumby).

It turned out the seller was a dealer whose son was a prominent showjumping rider. He would buy a batch of brumbies off the local sales, run them through a ring to see which ones might have had talent over jumps, and then advertise the rest. I was attracted by the price, as it would enable me to resell after breaking her in and add on the price of my labor.

When I visited the dealer, I picked out a smallish bay mare around 15h. Funnily, she'd had her mane clipped off, so I knew she'd been handled somewhat! He showed me how he caught her and tied her to a pole in the middle of a round ring. He'd hobbled her and clipped off her mane. I thought she certainly hadn't been handled in any conventional way, but I bought her and paid for her transport to our house.

The dealer never questioned my ability to handle the horse or what type of facility I had. He simply sold the horse so as to move on to the next one. In those days, I lived in the Adelaide outer suburbs, and the paddock I used was in the foothills, which is now part of a trail to Cleland Conservation Park, Mt Lofty, and about half a mile from where I lived.

It consisted of a large hill with a section at the top for grazing and the lower section covered in olive trees. There was a small flat area at the bottom where there was a trough and room to feed out. The whole area was fenced by two strands of barbed wire attached to droppers. It seemed to work; there again, I had no choice.

I suddenly realized that if I turned out this filly onto the 20 acres with the others, I would never catch her, and even worse, she might go through the fences! So, with this predicament in mind, I bought a neck strap. That was about $25, so I was already eating into my profit.

I still use it today, such was the sturdiness and quality.

The transport company unloaded her to our house and tied her to the stobie pole (telegraph pole) in our backyard. There, she remained tied up until I could work out what to do with her. I quickly found out I couldn't walk straight up to her, but considering I was her only source of food and water, she put up with me approaching her slowly. I put a towel on the end of a broomstick and stroked her with it until I was able to touch her all over.

Gradually, I was able to place my hands on her without her pulling back or kicking out, and indeed, she started to look forward to me doing it. She could eat while I would scratch or brush her all over.

After a while, I could lead her around the backyard (over Dad's lawn and stone paths) to my make-shift trough, so I didn't have to take a bucket to her any longer. What amazed me was this was all accomplished within a week.

Anyway, at that point, I decided she must go on the hill with the two others.

I didn't have a lot of trouble catching her, as it turned out. She became routined by the other horses coming down to the water and seeing me provide feed. Within a short while I'd taught her to lunge, and accept a roller and bit. I led her down the road with a saddle on off one of the other horses, and at some point, I climbed on her back.

It certainly wasn't formalized in any way, but by the end of the summer holidays, she was broken in, and I was riding her around the roads like any other broken-in horse.

After that, I had other unhandled horses, and they all broke in without much trouble.

What did I learn from this?

- Ask for more details when answering advertisements.

- You have to work at the horse's pace, which involves trial and error and a learning curve.

- I wasn't going to buy brumbies again without better facilities. It is better to buy a young 2-year-old from a breeder.

- I was trading my time for money, and frankly, there were better ways to make a profit.

- I survived!

Another unhandled horse

This time, it was my husband who bought the horse. Peter was inspired by Maurice Wright, who was demonstrating the Jeffery Method of horse handling around Australia. We had seen him in several demonstrations at interstate events, where he would take on an unhandled wild horse and break it in in front of an audience while explaining how he did it. He practiced the principles of Kel Jeffery, who first developed it and gave demonstrations up until he was an old man. Maurice wrote several books on the subject.

The Australian Stock Horse Society had only just formed, and Peter had formed the first branch in our State. So, we decided to invite Maurice over to do a demonstration as a fundraiser. We managed to find a filly off Anna Creek Station, which was sent down in a truck to the Adelaide Sales Pavilion at Wayville, where, before a huge crowd, Maurice began to show the method.

My husband, who was a professional photographer, photographed the whole demonstration. People were spellbound as this was something rarely seen: a man and a wild beast in a yard together, getting to know one another in the kindest possible way.

The filly was extra sensitive and reactive, showing the crowd that she was indeed an unhandled horse! We saw she was very determined, as she could bite, kick, and rear. We noted the filly watched him the entire time, and when licking her lips, Maurice explained it was a necessary sign before he moved on to anything further.

Maurice even apologized to the crowd that she was taking a lot longer than usual. They all said to carry on as they were enthralled.

All Maurice did, in effect, was to use a long rawhide rope with a ring attached, which was slipped around her neck. He would gently tug it with immediate release until she faced towards him, then back off. He called it "reward with retreat."

Slowly, this was built on until he could move up close, whereupon he would let her sniff him. As Maurice stated, the filly was the most difficult he had ever started; this stage took about an hour and a half, longer than the rest of the process put together.

In the next step, he started rubbing her all over in "advance and retreat" and waited for the lips-licking before advancing again. Within a short time, he'd managed to rub all over her, even between her back legs and lifting her tail. He then proceeded to mount and slide all over her body in the same "advance and retreat" manner.

He brought in a saddle cloth, rubbed it all over, and then proceeded in the same fashion with a saddle. He girthed up and walked away.

This was the only time he left the filly to herself. Soon enough, her attention left him, and she bucked her way around the ring, showing all the signs of a seasoned rodeo horse. When she finally stopped, Maurice walked back into the ring, picked up the rope, and proceeded as if nothing had happened. The mare immediately felt secure again.

Because she licked her lips quite a bit, some skeptics thought he must have had a trick, like honey!

To cut a long story short, Maurice had another man on horseback brought into the ring to achieve forward movement by leading her off it. As he explained, he'd spent all this time asking the horse to stand still. Now he wanted her to move! He rode her around the ring, and only after that did he slide off and bridle the horse. He asked for some bend from the reins on the ground. All this still with "advance and retreat."

She quickly learned to walk and trot around alongside the horse, at which point Maurice called it a day. The whole event took around 3 hours.
You can view a You-tube video of Maurice demonstrating the Jeffery Method with a young unhandled horse on his own property here:

https://jeanettegower.substack.com/publish/post/155000724

or here: https://youtu.be/jX1Q0QINfB4

So what happened to this horse after that? My husband looked at the photos that night and decided the mare had good enough conformation to buy her. He wanted to follow up with the Jeffery Method himself.

After buying her for $80, he went to the stables where she was located to pick her up. The man there warned him to be careful, as the method didn't work. He said he couldn't even get into the stable with her!

Fortunately, Peter had bought himself a long rawhide rope with a ring, the same as Maurice's. He spent an hour or so repeating everything to put her onto a truck. The man was totally shocked. As we didn't have yards, Peter brought her back to the neighbour's cattle yards. And there, the process began.

He called her Anna after Anna Creek Station. Within 3 weeks, he was riding her all around the property, doing obstacles and cracking a stock whip. He found her very smart and quick to learn but extremely sensitive and also ticklish. This was the reason she had been so difficult at the start. However, without the techniques of the Jeffery Method, both Peter and Maurice concluded she would have been very difficult to start by any other method.

Within a few months, Peter had her classified as an Australian Stock Horse and was riding her in ASH demonstrations without a bridle. After being ridden for several years, she was retired for breeding. Her sons and daughters won 5 Futurities and were multiple champions under saddle.

Peter and Anna pushing the tractor tyre

What did we learn from this?

- Anna would have been a tough horse under conventional methods. She was extra smart, though she lacked the extra ability to go with it. We needed to breed her to something with ability while toning down the re-activeness. This worked with all her progeny.

- All work had to be followed up. You can't treat a horse like it knows everything from day one. You have to repeat all the steps.

- The demonstration emphasized "advance and retreat." We still do it to this day. It is a very useful approach to all training, especially useful for difficult or sensitive horses.

- Trust is everything – if you want the horse to trust you, it is just as important that you trust the horse (and this means you must trust yourself!)

The problem (?) mare

I once bought a horse I'd admired locally. The mare was a nice strong type, showing a bit of Arab blood with nice neck and hindquarters. I was going to use her for riding and later breeding. When I collected her, I was told, "She doesn't tie up, so I tie her by the tail." I thought this to be rather odd, so I didn't take much notice of it. "She's not much good to ride; she doesn't *do* anything, so we bred from her. She also doesn't load very well in a float."

With that I proceeded to ride her the 10 miles or so home. She seemed a bit confused but we got there. I would tie her with a bit of string to one of the olive trees when I needed to groom and saddle her. After breaking it a few times she gave up and I never had any further trouble.

Next, I proceeded to try to find out her breeding. However, after making enquiries, I found out that she'd never been broken in. So this dear mare had been ridden off and on under the assumption that she had been. No wonder she knew nothing! I went back and started from the beginning and filled in the gaps. She became a pleasure to ride.

The time came when I had to transport her. Yes she would load, but would race out the back. In the process of trying, she ran under the closed tailgate and hit her rump very hard on it. She obtained a permanent dent on her hindquarters, just where the sacrum ends and the tailbone starts. From that moment, her tail was paralyzed. But she didn't try running out the back again!

The funny thing was she was in foal when that happened, so I later sent her to a stud to foal her down for me in case there were any issues. As the manager watched her foal, he heard a loud crack. Sure enough, her spine had shifted back into place, and she was able to move her tail again!

What did I learn from this?

- Don't believe everything someone tells you about a horse. They may not know. Research the history.

- Horses learn good and bad things, even when you're not trying to teach them anything. Always go back to the beginning.

- With a little patience, and by behaving calmly and casually, many problems simply disappear without you doing a lot to make it happen.

- Horses that are bought and sold again become more traumatized with each new home unless you recognize the signs. Take steps to rehabilitate them by building trust. Rushing this process doesn't work.

Buying a young horse: – Kate Collins

My search for my last horse would end up with me buying a 10 month old palomino young horse called "Chalani Monash" bred by Chalani Australian Stock Horses. Monash came into my life as a well built, intelligent, confident, calm temperament and a maturing height of 16 hands plus. Just exactly what I was looking for.

I found the breeder extremely knowledgeable, caring, and interested in the future I would be providing for Monash. I wanted a journey with a young horse from ground work to eventually having it started under saddle, and then on to Working Equitation competition, a partnership built on total respect and harmony.

Kim ensured Monash was taught to lead well, tie up, pick up feet, load, and travel well in a float before he left for my place in New South Wales. Interstate travel was also organized by Kim. Kim did a wonderful job ensuring I got the right young horse to suit my chosen Dressage and Working Equitation disciplines. Chalani Australian Stock Horses also offered after-purchase resources for the keeping and schooling of a young horse.

I never thought I would buy a horse from a breeder as it has and still does concern me the turnover of unwanted horses each year. In the past I have bought 3 horses from previous owners. They are all now happily retired with me.

........so why a change of heart for the purchase of my last horse?

- I did my homework and knew exactly what I was looking for; age, breed, temperament and height. I also knew now that I had the knowledge to school a young horse with compassion and patience.

- I wanted an uphill Heritage Stock Horse with 3 good paces. Intelligence and spark was a must. I also wanted to be able to research my horse's breed lines, especially the thoroughbred lines, out of interest.

- I didn't want to go through hundreds of "for sale ads" and deal with a multitude of people looking to sell their horse due to "no fault of it's own" or "looking for it's forever home."

- I found Chalani Monash online and I couldn't believe my good fortune to be honest. He was everything and more I wanted on my list. I boarded a plane and flew to South Australia to view him at the breeders stud. I also had the opportunity to view his sire and dam. I highly recommend being able to go to a stud and view other progeny as well. The rest is history.

What did I learn from this?

- Owning a young horse comes with a huge responsibility and cost.

- The personal rewards are absolutely wonderful.

- It's a journey of learning and personal goals reached every day.

Monash is now six years old, and I'm living *the Young Horse Dream*. He has been a dream come true and it is wonderful that the breeders have a continued interest in his progress. All because I *Bought The Right Horse* from a responsible breeder.

Buying a foundation mare – Skyview Stud

In 2010, my beautiful competition mare Goldmine Latte HSH (Lil) and I had a simple but very serious riding accident. At the time, the medicos said I would never be able to ride again, and Lil would never compete again, due to both of our head injuries.

I have loved dilute horses for my whole life, so we made the decision to switch to breeding, and find a second excellent quality broodmare. I was invited by Goldmine Stud, to look at a 4yo mare, as they were closing the stud due to ill health after 40 years of breeding. My very dear friend Lesley from Queensland, who also owned horses from this line (including Lil's full sister, Goldmine Figurine HSH) came with me.

When we arrived we viewed the 4yo, and then the owners suggested we meet her mother.

They led us to a set of yards, and there Blush was, in a canvas winter neck and body rug with only her head showing. She looked at me, as if to say "Thank goodness you're here. I've been waiting for you. Let's go home now", and I burst into uncontrollable sobs. The breeders took off her rugs, and as I ran my hands over her body, she put her head over my shoulder and drew me to her. I have never had such a reaction before or since.

We thought her price was an insane amount of money. I had never considered paying that amount of money, especially for a 19 year old horse. Nor did I think with a young family, we would even be able to consider it.

I thanked the breeders, and we left the property about an hour later. We went to McDonalds for a "late breakfast", and every time I mentioned Blush's name, I burst into ridiculous, uncontrollable sobs. Lesley agreed Blush was a significant amount of money, but "hardly ever in life, do you have an opportunity to purchase a mare of this quality," and from my response, "the Universe was trying to tell (me) something."

From a logical perspective, I knew Blush's lines intimately, having tracked Peter and Gail Rossington's Claredale Champagne Charlie HSH lines for more than 10 years, Blush was a Charlie daughter, out of a superbly bred mare. I'd owned Blush's daughter, Lil, from 7 months to 7years. She was the horse love of my life.

Blush (Goldmine Champagne Blush HSH) was also one of the two best performed and most awarded palomino mares in Australia, having won Melbourne Royal 7 years in a row, which has never been done before or since. Logically, Lesley and I agreed, if there was any mare that could help us achieve Skyview Stud's vision of breeding some of the best dilute riding horses in the country, Blush was it. As she was in foal, we decided if she had a filly, we could keep it. If she had a colt, we could sell it and recoup some of her purchase price.

For the next 10 days, every time I spoke of Blush, I broke down in tears. Seeing this, my partner said "Just buy her. We'll add her to the mortgage and pay her off over 5 years." We had Blush vet checked to confirm the pregnancy, and she came home.

From the moment she arrived, I never regretted purchasing her. It was absolutely joyous seeing her head over the gate waiting for me, every morning. She was incredibly breathtaking, an incredibly easy horse I had the pleasure of being guardian. No amount of money could make up for the way Blush could make you feel in her presence.

Five months later, Blush gave birth to a chestnut filly and the following year at 22 years old, Blush gave us a most beautiful buckskin filly Skyview Eternity HSH, her last foal. I also managed to secure a bulk amount of frozen semen from her only living stallion son, Goldmine Mirage HSH (cremello).

Blush was always The Queen. She was kind and loving, but had every other horse on the property in line, with just a minor flick of her ear. In 2013 when her paddock mate passed away from colic they both had 10 week old buckskin filly foals born 3 days apart. Blush did the most unbelievable thing, adopting her mate's filly and fed them both.

Both Goldmine Latte (Lil), and Skyview Eternity (Tilly), successfully competed with me, achieving many National, State and Royal Show Championships, Supreme Championships, Horse of the Year awards and Lifetime Awards. And best of all, we just "got each other."

As of 2025, a short 15 years later, Greg and I are incredibly blessed to be able to look across our paddocks at Skyview Stud, and see Blush's children, grand-children, and now, her first great grand-child, a beautiful 2yo buckskin filly we named Skyview Honour HSH, out of Skyview Champagne Grace HSH. We have been very fortunate (and worked very hard) to be able to retain the fillies that most captured our hearts. Goldmine Champagne Blush HSH will always be kept in the most special of places in our hearts.

What did I learn from this?

- It is very important to really like the individual horse and feel a connection to it. Horses are never easy, and a true connection will make the difficult times, much easier.

- View them in the flesh. Photos and videos are easily altered these days, and refer to point 1 for the importance of connection.

- Buy from proven lines. Lines you either have experience with and enjoy, or that someone who you know and trust has had personal, hands on experience with. And by proven lines, I mean the horse itself is proven, not just "2 generations back is a cousin of X who was related to Y."

- The initial purchase price in the scheme of things, is irrelevant (within reason). Especially when you're looking at riding 10+years or breeding 20-30 years, your time and enjoyment.

- If you can spend up to $30,000 to buy the horse you want for riding, it is better to do this than try and breed one "cheaply", especially if you have very specific criteria.

- Quality begets quality. That refers to mare *and* stallion. If you want an extraordinary foal, find an extraordinary mare, put her to the best complementary stallion you can find, and hope for the best. Buying an ordinary mare and putting her to an excellent stallion, is unlikely to give you what you want.

Buying a horse in utero – Mandy Evins

I've bought foals in utero before. I knew the drill. This time, the goal was clear: a high-class Hanoverian dressage horse, the kind with impeccable bloodlines, bred for performance, built for the long haul. Fillies were the dream. Geldings would be sold.

For 15 years, I'd worked with the same breeder. Seen the mares. Knew their care. No gamble. No guesswork. The stud was top-tier: in-vulva foaling alarms, in-house vet, the works. Nothing left to chance.

Why buy this way?

I wanted new bloodlines, a strategic move for my small stud. After years of research into imported lines, I settled on a Sezuan/RoyalClassic cross. This wasn't a random pairing; it was calculated. I grilled the seller with questions. I knew she'd visited the sire in Germany. She knew the temperament first hand. Temperament is very important to me.

Trust is everything. The bloodlines matter, but the breeder and the facilities do too. Read the fine print in the contract. In-utero deals often state colt option only. Sometimes, the reverse. It didn't matter to me. Competition first. Breeding second, if the quality was there. The foal came with a live-foal guarantee: must stand and nurse within 24 hours, with a vet certificate to back it up.

Pros:

- You can access better or different bloodlines than you can breed yourself.

- It is around the same price as buying a foal on the ground.

- Guaranteed that the foal is yours. Quality foals on the ground sell quickly.

- You don't have to foal down yourself and you have the Live Foal Guarantee if there are complications with the birth.

Cons:

- The wait is long. Painfully long.

- You're committed before you know what you're getting. Could be bigger, smaller, the wrong colour, or just not what you pictured.

My result? A powerful black colt with four white socks. Absolute standout with an elegant neck. From day one, I knew this was stallion material. Now maturing at 18h, that was not what I was expecting! I won't breed him though until he passes temperament and ride-ability tests for Hanoverian licensing. Responsible breeders don't breed *just because they can.*

Lessons Learned:

- Trust is king. Research the breeder, the bloodlines, the facilities. Don't cut corners.

- Quality over everything. Start at the top.

- Read every contract clause. Twice.

- Insurance. Non-negotiable. You own that foal from birth—including vet bills.

Would I do it again?

In a heartbeat!

Amanda Evins with HB Sezuantino. Photo: Sue Parkinson

My worst experience in buying a horse – Wendy Brown.

I made arrangements to travel interstate with two friends (my support team) to see a 4 yr old Warmblood mare for sale. Prior to leaving I had negotiated an agreed price.

After riding her I decided to buy her subject to a vet check and X-rays. That afternoon the owner contacted me to say she had been offered a higher price and would sell to the best offer. This did not impress me as the agreement had been made before making the costly trip.

Since we were staying till the next day I made arrangements to see the plan B horse which was not too far away. He seemed to be a reasonable prospect. However, that evening the first horse owner rang to say she would honour my original offer.

So I booked a vet check and X-rays to be done at the end of that week. After returning home I was notified the horse was lame due to an abscess and I would need to cancel the vet. A few days later I was told the horse had been sold.

Unimpressed with it all I asked the seller of plan B horse to book a vet check and X-rays. The vet reported he had a canker and would need 6 weeks of treatment. Once he was cleared I agreed to buy him and unfortunately didn't get the x rays done. On arrival he was lame and diagnosed with DJD (degenerative joint disease) by my vet. Long story short, after 9 months rest in the paddock he was still lame. Eventually he had to be put down.

Lesson learnt: Have X-rays – buyer beware~!

***

Chapter 14

Final thoughts

Trust your instincts, trust the process

A s we draw this journey to a close, let's take a moment to reflect on the path we've traveled together. From those tentative first steps of understanding your riding ambitions to the confident purchase of your new horse, this guide has aimed to provide you with a comprehensive roadmap. Each chapter has been crafted to equip you with insights and tools needed to make informed, confident decisions in horse buying and ownership.

Throughout this book, we've explored the importance of aligning your goals with the right horse, assessing types that fit your riding style, and understanding the intricacies of long-term investment and care. You've learned how to craft a personalized checklist, navigate the marketplace, and evaluate potential horses with a discerning eye. We've delved into recognizing warning signs, understanding legal aspects, and the nuances of negotiation, all components in ensuring a successful purchase.

Key takeaways have emerged that will serve you well on your journey. The importance of defining your ambitions cannot be overstated; clarity in what you seek sets the foundation for every decision.

Recognizing a horse's temperament and understanding how to match it with your own personality ensures a harmonious partnership. The value of detailed evaluations, both behavioral and physical, safeguards against unforeseen challenges and enhances confidence in your choices. These insights, paired with a solid grasp of market dynamics and legal frameworks, empower you to make decisions in keeping with your goals and lifestyle.

I encourage you to take these lessons and apply them in your own horse-buying endeavors. Approach each decision with the confidence that comes from knowledge and preparation. Remember, each purchase is not simply a transaction but an opportunity for growth and learning.

Ashton Ide and his ASH mare, Hvirfs Gracious. Choosing the right horse means both horse and rider can learn and have fun together.

Every horse I have ever bought has taught me something.

As you can see, from a young teenager without parents to support my "hobby," I had to do everything by myself. This taught me resilience and adaptability. I certainly didn't do anything by the book (least of all the processes in *this* book), but I had the ingenuity to problem solve and ask questions of others.

You don't need to do it this way either, but I am sure you will choose better horses, make better decisions, and have better options if you do.

You can embrace the process, knowing that you are equipped with the tools to succeed. Only you can take action.

Remember you must choose a horse with which you can develop a bond. Otherwise, you will lose motivation to hang out with it, enjoy its talents, try new opportunities, and generally have fun with it. If you don't enjoy your horse, why would you own it?

Beyond the purchase, commit to continuous growth and engagement in the equestrian community. Share your experiences, learn from others, and contribute to a culture of support and knowledge. The community offers a wealth of expertise and camaraderie that enriches your journey. Whether through local clubs, online forums, or mentorship, your involvement will deepen your understanding and foster lifelong friendships. And enhance your enjoyment of your horse!

It's been a privilege to share my passion and knowledge with you, drawing from over 50 years of experience. As you embark on or continue your horse-buying adventure, I am confident that you will find fulfillment in the process. Celebrate each moment, from the simple pleasure of a quiet trail ride to the thrill of mastering new skills with your horse.

For each successful buyer, the horse finds the best possible home. That's the reason I write. ~ Jeanette

If you liked what you read, please share your feedback with me. I would love to hear about your experiences buying your dream horse!

"The journey of a thousand miles begins with a single step." In the world of horse ownership, each step you take is an opportunity to build a rewarding partnership.

Trust in your abilities, remain open to learning, and remember that the bond you create with your horse is as unique as it is enriching.

Here's to your continued success and enjoyment in the equestrian world.

***

Share Your Thoughts and Help Others Find Their Dream Horse

Now that you have everything you need to **embark on your horse-buying journey**, it's time to pass the reins and help others navigate theirs!

By sharing your honest opinion of *Buy the Right Horse* on Amazon, you'll guide other **keen horse buyers** to the information they need to make confident, informed decisions.

Your review is more than just feedback—it's a way to pass on your newfound knowledge and keep the joy of responsible horse ownership alive. Together, we can inspire a new generation of riders, breeders, and horse lovers to find the perfect equine partner.

Thank you for helping to keep this dream alive. The horse-buying journey is made better when we share what we've learned—and with your review, you're helping us do just that.

Click here to leave your review on Amazon

QR CODE HERE

Patience with your new horse

When you buy a new horse, be patient

Just be patient – Lee McLean, Keystone Equine (with permission).

We've found with all the horses we've brought in over the years that mentally and/or physically, they are adjusting for the better part of one full year. At least.

This is why all our sale horses and ponies come with a one-year guarantee that they will fit in and be able to do the job for their new people. Because if not (and it does happen to well-prepared horses and to good people), we want our homesick horse to come back home to us.

We will regroup, wait to find his level and if the stars align, we will try again. Some very knowledgeable horse(wo)men will scoff at this notion of a horse needing this amount of time to settle in. They will cite that they have client horses who are showing at a high level, traveling constantly, changing hands all of the time. I would point out that these horses are very accepting, to the point of being stoic.

This does not in any way mean that they are happy, living their best life, or exuberant! Ah, yes. Let's admit it. There are many times when sparkling joy is more an inconvenience than a blessing, when it comes to managing our horses. I get that. I understand. Anyway, some very good horses will go off the rails a bit, when changing homes and methodology in their handling. As would any one of us, if we were honest.

Others will take up as little space as possible, doing their utmost to blend in. They might go on for months, before the 'company manners' wear off. Some will go beautifully in new hands, winning and making friends,but they aren't eating well. They are standing as though carved in stone, not engaging in the hustle and bustle around them, nor are they interacting with other horses.

It takes a sharp eye to see what is really going on with anew horse. Most will do their best to try and please us but I would like to remind you, if you have been so blessed as to have a new face greeting you over the gate, to give your newcomer the benefit of the doubt.

Start carving out a routine. Please, don't go changing the turnout patterns, the type of bit, the discipline, the feed, the number of times he (or she) is ridden, right away. Do your best to replicate the horse's prior life, for a while... unless it is one that was riddled with abuse or neglect, of course.

So often, when a horse changes hands, the new owner or trainer will immediately begin changing him. Making him into something else. They'll start rebuilding his posture, changing his way of going, trying new bits, putting him on different feed—at the same time as the horse has received a vetting, a new farrier, therapeutic bodywork, an overdue dental visit,perhaps—and while understandable, it's too much, too soon.

Every little thing from how we bed and blanket, to how we approach and halter them, whether or not we feed treats, what sort of riding we do in what surroundings and weather, how we load into what sort of trailer, how we fit a saddle, how we saddle up, mount up and warm up... all will be different with every one of us.

We will all mean well and strive to do the best for our horses, but we will be different. Whether or not a horse will be homesick—aka grieving—has nothing to do with the level to which he has been trained! Maybe,read that one again.

So, be the patient partner, the rock. Watch your new horse and be willing to consider what he has to say. Remember, you liked him well enough as he was, or you wouldn't have bought him in the first place! Figure out what he is telling you, what he likes and what worries him.

Go slowly but surely into new territory, for you are maybe wanting to do things that are fun and comfortable for you, but for him, have stayed shrouded in mystery, on the dark side of the moon. You can have goals for the future but please, be willing to share the discomfort your new horse is feeling in the now. Prioritize these little changes that will add up to make him truly your partner.

Realize that even if things are going smoothly between you, there will be hurdles and challenges in his social order, as he makes his way within his new herd. Be watchful for signs of ongoing bullying, because this can make everything else in the new horse's life extra hard.

If this is the case, try to find him a group of horses that are low-key, low-energy and forgiving of strangers. If he is unusually large or small, or very young or old, these, alone, will require you to be more observant and caring during this critical time.

Note that our horses can change places easier if their people and programs stay the same; they can change key people more easily, if they remain in the same surroundings. It is the overall, straight-across-the-board shift that can un-moor any horse. Outbursts in the new horse are so often emotional in origin, rather than caused by physical discomfort, or downright pain.

This is why so many times, we feel we've been sold a horse who was misrepresented, that we've been somehow duped. "This is NOT the same horse I rode in the trial!" we think. We are right, of course, for he terribly changed. We're quick to blame the seller, rather than question the fluid emotional state of our new purchase.

While I usually proceed with a new horse just as I mean to go on, I will be paying attention. I won't be barging ahead, dragging this confused horse along behind me. Nor, will I be letting him 'settle in' by putting him on the back burner, untouched. There is a balance to be found.

If you are purchasing, leasing or boarding a new horse, please make space in your heart for a sentient being who will often be homesick, even if you have the feeling that you are making his life better. You may even well be rescuing him and yet...In the new horse's eyes, you have turned his life—that is, all that he knew for sure and could anticipate—completely upside-down."

***

Order The Thinking Horse Breeder and other books direct from the author:

https://thinkinghorsebreeder.chalani.net/

or overseas: https://books.by/jeanette-gower

About the Author

Jeanette Gower's decades of experience span muddy paddocks, long nights foaling, and enough saddle time to write a book (literally). Based on the practicalities of horse care and breeding, Jeanette has made it her mission to help people make better decisions around horse ownership, from buying the right horse to building a lifelong partnership based on trust, ethics, and a lifetime of being around them.

Jeanette's approach is grounded in responsible horse ownership. *Buy the Right Horse* is her way of cutting through the fluff and guiding readers toward thoughtful, informed decisions. It's not about chasing ribbons or quick fixes; it's about making choices that prioritize the welfare of the horse and build stronger partnerships.

Jeanette is a voice of reason in an industry often clouded by trends and misconceptions. She advocates for transparency in breeding practices, ethical horse sales, and ongoing education for owners, because, as she says, "the learning never stops."

Her writing style blends hard-earned wisdom with an approachable tone, making complex ideas digestible for readers of all levels; expect practical advice delivered with a few home truths.

Jeanette's philosophy? "Think before you buy. Think harder before you breed."

She believes in building confidence through knowledge. Her work encourages readers to embrace both the highs and the challenges of horse ownership with eyes wide open. She's not afraid to call out poor practices, but she does so with the heart of a mentor, offering actionable solutions.

Her deep commitment to horse welfare shines through in every anecdote, every lesson, and every strong opinion she shares, because when it comes to horses, there's no room for half measures.

So whether you're a first-time buyer or a seasoned breeder looking for a fresh perspective, Jeanette invites you to join her journey toward more mindful, meaningful horse ownership. After all, as she's fond of saying, "Every horse tells a story - the horse is a reflection of *you*."

Contact the Author:

If you enjoyed reading this book, I would be really grateful if you could put a Review on Amazon. Just search Amazon - books - *Buy the right horse* and follow the prompts. To buy *signed* copies, or for answers to general queries about horse breeding or buying, I can be contacted via *The Thinking Horse Breeder* Facebook page or https://thinkinghorsebreeder.chalani.net/or jeanette.gower@gmail.com

Contact the Stud:

Chalani can be contacted by email chalani@chalani.net or our Facebook page. At stud: Chalani Sunstream HSH is available by frozen semen in USA, and Australia. Photos and video on the *Chalani* Facebook page, the *Chalani* website or You-tube channel.

Join me on Substack:

For my regular weekly blog and podcast. https://jeanettegower.substack.com/

REFLECTIONS ON 50+YEARS OF HORSE BREEDING

Tired of theoretical advice & generic tips? Ask questions. Get insights, practical advice, resources, & inspiration. Master the art, science & tools for excellence from a seasoned horse breeder who's been in the trenches.

Launched 2 years ago

Type your email...   Subscribe

Also by Jeanette Gower

The Thinking Horse Breeder

Horse breeding is more complex than you think. Set yourself up to succeed in your passion for horses. Are you breeding horses and want to take it to the next level? Do you want to make better choices, breed better horses, improve your results? How would you go about establishing a horse stud?

It can be a lonely journey without someone to learn from, to show you how to lessen the mistakes along the way, and to steer you in the right direction. *The Thinking Horse Breeder* is a step by step, treasure trove of practical information for those who want to thrive and succeed doing what they love.

This book discusses selection of foundation stock, planning matings, breeding methods, genetic diseases, conformation and temperament, foaling down, raising foals, young horse training, common problems, financials, promotion, photography and ethical considerations, in an easy-to-read, authentic style.

Each chapter can be read and re-read for new insights. It will challenge your thinking and give you the art, science and tools for success. Everything you need to know is here in a simple, non-technical format based on the author's experiences and reflections over 50+ years. For aspiring, hobby or serious, established breeders, this will be an invaluable guide to be read over and over, so you too can master the inevitable challenges and be successful.

Order The Thinking Horse Breeder

and other books direct from the author:

https://thinkinghorsebreeder.chalani.net/

Other countries: https://books.by/jeanette-gower

See my ebooks here:

https://jeanettegower.gumroad.com/

www.ingramcontent.com/pod-product-compliance
Lightning Source LLC
Chambersburg PA
CBHW071523120626
46550CB00006B/2332